Are You a Mule or a Queen?

Are You a Mule or a Queen?

*How to Have
Others Honor
Your Wishes and
Value Your Time*

Lisa Blackwell

LANGDON STREET PRESS

Langdon Street Press
212 3rd Avenue North, Suite 290
Minneapolis, MN 55401
612.455.2293
www.langdonstreetpress.com

ISBN - 978-1-936183-48-7
ISBN - 1-936183-48-x
LCCN - 2010933662

Cover Design and Typeset by Nate Meyers

Printed in the United States of America

Acknowledgements

I would like to thank my two writing buddies, Karen S. Williams and Harriet Washington, for encouraging me to keep writing when the times got lonely or frustrating. I would like to thank my father for always being supportive in my pursuit of various career paths. Many thanks to Dr. A. Walker for engaging in stimulating conversation that produced a lot of vibrant ideas. Most of all, thank God for giving me the hope and the courage to write on a subject that may help women get the equable treatment and respect they deserve.

Contents

Introduction

Do you ever feel like you're getting the life sucked out of you by friends, family, or coworkers who supposedly "care"? If you do, you're not alone. Though they may not speak about it, many women feel this way. Most women, in fact, have a natural instinct to nurture, but this characteristic sometimes gets them into trouble. Historically, we have often ended up divorced, with empty nests, underpaid, fatigued, lonely, and depressed. Ultimately, who has to take responsibility when we end up in a place we don't want to be? We do.

For many years during my career, I was an executive coach and process specialist. Part of my charter was advising people how to work more efficiently with very little time and resources available. Often, when I started working with them on efficiency, they would open up about being overburdened by personal commitments other than work. Commonly, one of the reasons these people were pressed for time was that, outside of work, others monopolized their time and energy without considering the individual's schedule and needs.

Most of the folks I coached wanted someone to listen to them and consider their needs. I also noticed that women generally seemed more pressed for time than men. Women had so many obligations outside of work—children, parents, girlfriends, church, charities, and so on—that many of them seemed burnt out and joyless. I met many older women who described dark lives that were full of burdens and duties. For them the only sunshine was the innocence and hope their children showed. Even in the twenty-first century, with all the technology, education, and open dialogue on popular talk shows, there are still many women whose friends or family are not treating them considerately or compassionately. These women belong to all economic classes and educational groups. I know exactly how they feel because, secretly, I was also one of them.

I was raised to get an education and a good job, but self-care is something I had to learn on my own and through teaching others who, by society's standards, were successful. Many of these people, though prosperous in their careers, also had issues related to caring for themselves both inside and outside of work.

When I realized other people were in the driver's seat, controlling my spare time and creative energy, I knew I had to make a change. I felt my life was being wasted satisfying the emotional and intellectual needs of others. I felt cheated, since people were taking my time and ideas but very few were reciprocating. I decided to apply some of my process expertise to gathering data and analyzing why so many women, including me, seemed so overburdened.

In this book, I examine openly and nonjudgmentally many taboo situations in which women allow themselves to be exploited. I also consider issues ranging from family demands and inconsiderate, selfish friendships to parasitic husbands and boyfriends to establish the root causes and provide action-oriented solutions.

This book is meant to be a resource for those of you who seek ways to prevent people from casually mistreating you. The focus is on moving forward and growing, rather than clinging to a past spent struggling for respect. It will give you strategies for taking care of yourself and protecting your time.

My passion about this topic comes from having met many women with a poor quality of life, as well as my personal experience of reclaiming my life and time from those who assumed my life was at their disposal. My desire is to bring out of the shadows any behaviors that may not be serving you well so you can free up your time and energy and invest it in your own dreams.

Chapter 1:

Mules and Queens

A mule has neither pride of ancestry nor hope of posterity.

Robert Green Ingersoll

Have you ever wondered why some women become overburdened and exploited, while others are treated like royalty? Have you noticed that some women look happy and composed, while others look overweight and tired, as if they might keel over from a heart attack any second? Do you spend a lot of time listening to your family and friends tell drama-filled stories, when you'd rather be sleeping? Do people ask you to do a lot of things you don't want to do? Are people oblivious of how you feel when they talk to you? Do people treat you with honor and respect, or do they act as if your sole purpose in life is to validate them and make their lives easier? The pivotal question here is: are you treated like a mule or a queen?

Contrary to popular belief, there are mules and queens across all educational and social classes. There are incredibly wealthy "mules" in high society whose time and money are used up by friends and loved ones. Similarly, there are women who are queens in lower levels of society who subsist on meager incomes but whose families and friends love, cherish, and protect them. For the purposes of this book, the classification is based on how you are treated, as opposed to the material wealth you possess.

What are the characteristics of a mule? Wikipedia gives the following definition:

> Operators of working animals generally find mules preferable to horses: mules show less impatience under the pressure of heavy weights, and their skin, harder and less sensitive than that of horses, renders them more capable of resisting sun and rain.

Does this animal sound as if it has much fun in life? Are you similar to the mule because you are constantly being pressurized to take on the heavy burdens of others? Women who have become mules have tougher skin. They have endured more. Many have seen their mothers treated harshly and have come to expect nothing better.

The Webster Online definition of a "queen" is as follows:

a. A woman eminent in rank, power, or attractions <a movie *queen*>
b. A goddess or a thing personified as female and having supremacy in a specified realm
c. An attractive girl or woman; *especially*, a beauty contest winner

I conducted a short survey of thirty-five women between the ages of thirty and ninety-four, including both professionals and stay-at-home wives. I asked them one simple question: Other than receiving material gifts, what treatment or behavior makes you feel cared for like a queen?

Their individual responses were categorized as follows:

- Thoughtful acts from others: 15 responses
- Being recognized: 5 responses
- Others calling and checking in on them: 4 responses
- Making them feel secure: 4 responses
- Being listened to: 4 responses
- Being surprised: 3 responses

The following are some of the actual responses to the question "What treatment makes you feel cared for or like a queen?"

- "When you are sick and they [family] do things like give you breakfast."
- "When my husband is kind to relatives even though they may be a pain."
- "Kids cleaning for mom."
- "Knowing that your husband is taking responsibility for choices and actions, looking out for the family's well-being."
- "Knowing you have been heard. Others caring about what you are feeling."
- "Having a friend of thirty-five years calling to check in once a week."
- "Getting acceptance and recognition from people at work."

There are many factors that influence the way you are treated: your physical appearance, race, education, inter-personal skills, decision-making skills, how you articulate your thoughts, etc. Some are not within our immediate control; some are. In this book, we will discuss the factors you can change to increase the likelihood of being treated more like a queen.

Women have been raised and socialized to take care of others. Due to the patriarchal nature of society throughout history, inequality among the sexes has prevailed, giving woman less of a voice in the world. Before the civil rights and women's movements of the 1970s, women were only admitted into occupations that primarily involved taking care of others. These caregivers included nurses, teach-ers, secretaries, nannies, maids, and cooks. Thanks to pioneers such as Susan B. Anthony, Betty Friedan, and Martin Luther King Jr., who worked to turn the tables on discrimination against women, new, fairer norms were es-tablished to rebalance the status quo between the genders. Now, however, women have more choices, but many don't use the full range available to them.

Some young women fresh out of college make a vari-ety of choices before settling for one they feel suits them best. Other women wait until their children are grown up and out of the house before pursuing options that were not available to them when they were raised. Some women only give themselves the right to make their own deci-sions when they are in their sixties and seventies and the end of their lives is on the horizon.

Unfortunately, some women exercise very few op-tions to improve their lives, so they remain stuck. They often stay married to insensitive, cruel men. They be-come moms only and nothing else. They don't go back to school to open up income opportunities or meet new people with fresh ideas. Instead, they bury themselves in narrow-minded religious beliefs, closing themselves off to new points of view.

Even if you asked the most hardcore feminist whether she would like to be treated like a queen, she would say yes. Housewives and executives alike do not want to think of themselves as being overburdened and underappreciated, even though both groups of women wear hard work like a badge of honor.

So, how can you tell whether you are a mule or a queen? Take a look at the following fifteen questions:

- Are you the type of person who babysits, pet sits, and runs errands for friends, but then finds they are missing in action or make excuses when you need their help?
- Do you listen to your family and friends rattle on and on about their problems on the phone when you could be resting or doing household chores?
- Do you volunteer to help out of guilt and not pleasure?
- Do you loan men or family members money and worry about getting it back?
- Do you loan money to family when you have outstanding bills to pay?
- Do you let people say insensitive things to you without saying anything back?
- Do you drive more to see people than those same people drive to see you?
- Do you entertain family and friends at your home, even though they rarely reciprocate?

- Do you help organize church events more than anybody else?
- Have you not taken a solo vacation in years?
- Has a significant other you stayed with ever cheated on you—and blamed you?
- Do friends or family constantly want you to finance their great ideas?
- Do your parents or relatives manipulate you by whining or making you feel you are competing with other relatives for their affection?
- Do people freely criticize your lifestyle and marital status even though you haven't said anything about theirs?
- Have you scheduled or needed surgery and worried who would volunteer to take care of you?

If you answered yes to five or more of these questions, you allow people to overburden you without regard for your time or well-being. The following are some things the women I interviewed said made them feel like queens. How many of these have you experienced in the past six months?

- Has anybody taken you out to dinner?
- Did any of your friends remember your birthday without being prompted?
- Has anyone done something for you without being asked?
- Has anyone written you a thank-you email or handwritten note in the past year?
- Has anyone called to ask how you were feeling/doing over the past month without needing something?

• Has a friend or relative made you a home-cooked meal in the past month?

Ironically, a woman can be treated like a queen in some areas of her life (e.g., home, work, social circles, and secondary family situations) and like a mule in others. Being treated like a mule in one area is easily corrected, though. If she is treated like a mule in several or all areas, she may be heading for days of despair due to her inability to set appropriate boundaries. This may require the immediate intervention of a professional psychologist to prevent her from getting dragged under emotionally.

A prime example of this is single women whose families of origin demand a lot of their money and time. They may still have the everyday stress of caring for their own children. These women, often well educated, may be high fliers at work, but their personal stress often begins to bleed over into their work life. This can cause missed deadlines, which can lead to longer hours, reprimands from management, and missed promotions. The ultimate domino effect of these events is damaged self-esteem and a stagnant income. When such a woman's economic situation becomes tenuous, threatening the welfare and stability of herself and her family, she runs the risk of being manipulated in several areas of her life without a chance of reprieve.

Some factors have contributed to increasing the odds that contemporary women may have a higher probability of becoming a mule than becoming a queen. The first factor is physiological wiring. Because women tend to be right-brained creatures, we tend to focus on "feelings and creativity," so anything that tends to focus on negative feelings may prompt us to overanalyze without taking action. Instead of seeing unfairness and eliminating its source, we tend to ask "why?" too much. This hesitancy and contemplation may increase the odds of inequitable treatment.

Historically, women have been both patronized and protected. Until the late twenty-first century, women were programmed to follow a man's lead. This held true across the whole spectrum of behavior in relationships between the sexes, from waiting to be kissed, to waiting for a man to make the next move, to waiting to be asked to marry. Women were the passive ones in the relationship while men played dominant, and often domineering, roles. Basically, social programming sent a clear message to women to "keep your mouth shut and do what I tell you to do," whatever that happened to be. Even though women have been liberated, the residue of this social programming still remains in some women.

Certain structures support this subordination, and some organizations have historically assumed that a woman is married to the primary breadwinner, which may cause some management to pay her less than her male equivalents.

What makes matters more difficult is the fact that a lot of us are self-sabotaging. We don't need anybody else's help to mess us up. Women subordinate themselves sometimes (for example, waiting for men to approach them for a date). While there is a small subset of women who will approach men for a date, they are not the majority. Some women purposely subordinate themselves to get help ("I don't understand this computer—can you help me?"). Playing dumb and acting helpless to get help is clearly still a tool some women use.

Any social revolution where individuals in groups are expected to evolve from one role to another is never simple or painless. Because a social revolution requires institutions to change, it also requires individuals' cultural views of themselves to change. Extreme changes by a woman may cause discomfort for the individual's family, friends, and community, and fear of this inconvenience may cause her to hesitate or abandon her new course of action.

In any historically oppressed group, there are certain attractive aspects of being oppressed. For example, the old cliché that "women have the right to change their minds" was a very popular notion at one time. This meant basically that since you were oppressed, you were viewed as a child and were not responsible for your actions; you were allowed to be inaccurate. Unfortunately, there are very real consequences to propagating this stereotype. Because this cliché viewed a woman as a child, it allowed entities to take power from women while offering them an excuse to justify any irresponsible acts they may have committed.

In the old days, some women would say, "You got me pregnant!" This comment implied that a woman had no say in the act. She was just there as if she were an inanimate object. This excused a woman from taking responsibility, and it allowed her to blame another person. It is assumed the woman did not have the intellectual capability to recognize the consequences of her actions. The moment a woman gives her power away, how can she get it back? The bottom line is that women cannot have it both ways. You can't play both sides, since that destroys your credibility.

All your life, you may have been told that you are a woman and should, therefore, be loved and taken care of. But, at the same time, you want respect and the opportunity to do what men have traditionally done with regard to authority and power in personal relationships. The two roles can't be easily reconciled. One role requires you to be passive, and the other aggressive. These can't coexist for every role (i.e., spouse, lover, friend, employee). You can't mix and match roles so easily; you can't be passive as the lover but dominant as the head of the household. Women often try to pick and choose where they want to apply one role as opposed to another, but that often doesn't make sense.

Women have to find a balance. They have to have a discussion with the people in their lives—husband, friends, family, church, work, neighborhoods, and organizations—about the significance of striking this balance. Women may have to do a better job compartmentalizing their roles (e.g., being a high-powered attorney at work but not bringing all of that power and aggression into the household).

Black professional women have been particularly bitten by the results of not being able to compartmentalize their roles. Due to socioeconomic factors, black women head the household more often than in other cultures. That increases the likelihood that they will be under significant stress with demanding jobs that may not pay enough to support a family. But the status of being the primary breadwinner does not free them from doing traditional domestic duties their culture raised them to perform. Thus, you have a group of women who are more likely to be overloaded, which perhaps contributes to the higher divorce rates among blacks (Bianchi & Spain, 1986; Epanshade, 1985).

Women have to be acutely aware of the cost of the power role. Women may want the jobs and prestige men have, but they must understand the cost of these choices, because what feminism didn't tell them is that there is no free lunch.

Sometimes, a woman has to take action to be treated like a queen rather than make excuses for others who treat her disrespectfully. Many women are prone to look the other way and ignore bad behavior. They explain away shoddy treatment by their kids, friends, husbands, siblings, lovers, and colleagues. Greg Behrendt and Liz Tuccillo, who wrote *Sex and the City,* highlighted this fact in their book, *He's Just Not That into You: The No-Excuses Truth to Understanding Guys.* The book discusses women who refuse to face the reality about men who disappear after only a few dates or who didn't want to be bothered with them at all. This book shows that many women have a hard time holding men accountable for disrespectful treatment in the early stages of a relationship. What do you think happens when they have to deal with someone they have a longer history with? Many women would let the shared times cloud their judgment when it comes to asserting themselves in order to receive fair treatment.

Because others won't take responsibility for their unhappiness, women have to take ownership of their own happiness. This means being a full-fledged adult and taking risks. Letting family and friends make your decisions sets you up for disappointment and possible abandonment when things go wrong. Since many people will not own the bad results of what they told you to do, it will all be on you. Don't live out someone else's dreams. They had their chance; this is yours.

In this book, we will examine the different types of mule behaviors exhibited by women. While the subject matter can be applicable to men, the focus is on scenarios women typically encounter. For each mule behavior, we will also examine how a woman treated like a queen would respond to the same scenario. The road to being treated like a queen may be long, and it may require difficult behavior changes and boundary-setting, but it is the best road possible, especially considering the alternative.

Chapter 2:

Single Professional Women: Perfect Candidates For Mulehood

There are people who so arrange their lives that they feed themselves only on side dishes.

Jose Ortega y Gasset

The shows *Ally McBeal* and *Sex and the City* made single, professional working women appear to have lots of fun, friends, and dating prospects. Some single, professional women actually do enjoy an active social life; however, there is a dark side to being a professional woman. Although her lack of family may enable her to have more discretionary income and spare time at her disposal than women with families, these attributes can also attract personal parasites—family and friends who would like to overburden single professional women with problems, such as financial issues and relationship stresses. Thus, this type of professional woman, with all her talent, energy, and education, can morph into a mule without even knowing it. A single professional woman who is a mule can be easily manipulated and "operated" by others who have their own hidden agendas.

Since society has traditionally viewed single or older women as caregivers, people automatically assume they should be available to help when needed. Most women have a nurturing spirit, and when this need is not met by having a partner or kids, these women may get drawn into providing support for friends and family. The demands may at times be unfair, but the single, professional woman feels guilty about saying no and may be trying to avoid the pangs of loneliness.

Some examples of this are single professional women who "live" in the church. Many women spend their spare time volunteering there without developing their own interests. They also get caught up in counseling their other single girlfriends who exercise poor judgment and get into one bad relationship after another. They may get pressured to pay household bills, fund college tuitions, make car payments, and pay legal bills for troubled relatives, including nieces and nephews. These personal parasites zap the life out of the single professional woman, who herself often has no one to lean on for support. Personal parasites can feel particularly entitled if the single professional woman works in the same city where she grew up. This easy access makes it a breeze for the parasitic relatives or friends to pressure the woman in person.

How do we view older single women who have never been married and have no children? Society generally views them as not having any "real" reason to spend their money. There is also the assumption that they are lonely because it is believed that a woman needs something to love. This translates into the belief that she should be very glad to help family, friends, or community if help is needed.

There is also the idea that single women save the money they earn, so it accumulates. Since she is single there is no one to spend it on, so family members and friends think, "why not help me out?" Also, the probability gets higher if the single professional woman's family of origin is poor or if she has siblings who have not climbed the economic ladder to success.

Take Brittany, for example. She was one of five siblings. She studied hard enough to get a scholarship in architectural design. Even though she was a student, her family believed she had money as if she were already working. Her mother and sisters started leaning on her for scholarship money even before she graduated. She often complained that she felt like a bank due to her family's constant requests for monetary help. Personal parasites don't really feel much guilt about taking advantage of others. They just know you have it and they want it. The following definition of a parasite comes from Merriam-Webster Online:

a. A person who exploits the hospitality of the rich and earns welcome by flattery
b. Something that resembles a biological parasite in dependence on something else for existence or support without making a useful or adequate return

Some wording clearly stands out in the above definition—"dependence" and "support without making a useful or adequate return."

How many working professional women really thought, when they were studying in college, that if they could just earn an A in that class, they could get someone to be dependent on them later? How many graduation speakers say, "Go out into the world and make as many people dependent on you as you can"? This dependence may happen due to the parasitic nature of the woman's friends and family, but this is not what she would have consciously planned.

The popular slang term "being played" or "getting played" means that someone has charmed you or "blown your head up" with compliments and then taken advantage of you. One of the above definitions says a parasite "earns welcome by flattery." In "keeping it real" terms, this means you have been played. When people play you, they are purposely trying to put you into the "mule" category to get something they want.

How many times have you said "I know they are being nice because they want something" or "They never call me unless they want something"? I think most women have had these thoughts.

On the flip side, some people treat their female family members very well. Reisa was an only child whose parents had her late in life. When she was in grad school, her mother and father would go grocery shopping for her in their hometown and bring food to her on campus. Whenever she got sick, they would rush to pick her up and take her home so they could wait on her until she was feeling better. Her parents always made sure she had enough money on campus and did not lack any basic convenience. She often said she appreciated her parents because "they treated me like a queen" whenever she needed something. This may have had something to do with the 3.9 GPA she had when she graduated.

We've talked a little about how family members take advantage of single, professional women. We've also talked about an example of a woman who had a very nurturing family. Now, let's talk about women with spouses and boyfriends.

Bebe is an example of a woman who allowed herself to be turned into a mule by her boyfriend, Andy. Bebe earned top grades in high school and wanted to go on to study civil engineering at a large state university. Bebe was also very attractive, which ensured she attracted a lot of interest from the guys on campus. One of them, Andy, sized Bebe up and thought she would be an excellent asset as a girlfriend. He chased her down and eventually won her over with lots of promises and flattery. Andy's studies weren't going so well; in fact, he was very near flunking out. Maybe this pressure made him become even more infatuated with Bebe, and he finally asked her to marry him.

Andy had another hobby—playing with a band at night to earn some spare change. When he officially flunked out of school, he decided to tour with the band, hoping that one day soon he would hit the big payday. Andy convinced Bebe to hold down their apartment and pay most of the bills while he went from city to city. This went on for about three years without the band experiencing much success.

Bebe went on to graduate, landing a great job with a small local design firm and earning a nice salary. Reality began to hit Andy when the band's earnings could not ensure the future he wanted. He convinced Bebe to help support him while he went back to school. On the surface, this seemed like a good partnership. However, Andy was overly enamored by all the coeds he saw on campus. Though Bebe was paying his tuition and bills, he didn't stay faithful to her. He would hit on the smart girls in his class he thought would listen to his "woe is me" stories. He also said Bebe didn't understand him and that he wanted to leave her when he graduated. Every time there was a campus party at one of his study buddy's houses, he would bring Bebe along. She would be all smiles to everyone because she didn't have a clue about how Andy was creeping around behind her back.

Eventually Andy's juggling became apparent at home, and the couple started getting into verbal fights. Andy continued his studies and spent more time than necessary on campus. He even said he was considering leaving Bebe once he graduated but didn't want to pay her for financing his education. After graduating, Andy received an offer to work at a booming technology company in a growing beach town. Bebe decided to follow him soon after. She felt it would give them a fresh start and she decided to stick with the marriage. She quit her job, relocated to the town where Andy's job was, and took a job with a lower salary.

Bebe had become a mule to Andy and his dishonest behavior. She ignored the disrespect he showed her. After Andy got his first well-paying job out of college, not even a year had passed before she discovered him buying lingerie for a female coworker. What made matters worse was that Bebe was pregnant with their first child. She stayed with Andy after the birth of the baby and even had a second child by Andy. She didn't divorce him until twelve years later, spending most of those years in misery and denial. Bebe can't fully blame Andy. She was a complicit mule, subjugated by Andy's immature antics. She should have left before she introduced two innocent children into the mix.

Unlike Bebe, there are women who are able to pick loyal and loving people to surround them. Sarah was one of those women. She married Eric when they were both in their early twenties. After Eric graduated from a prestigious military academy and returned from the Vietnam War, they set up house together. They were both struggling to find employment and there wasn't enough money to cover basic household necessities. Eric said, "I love my wife because, in those early days of our marriage, we were very poor. We pretty much subsisted on crackers and water the first year. She stuck with me during those hard times, and I will never forget that. Now that I am more successful, I make sure she gets anything she wants."

Eric knew the value of a good woman. His career continued to flourish. He went on to run a branch of a major technology company and has done very well. Sarah doesn't have to work, and he makes sure she is taken care of. She gets treated like a queen because she chose to marry someone who valued her.

Some husbands feel an obligation to consult with their wives before making decisions. Some of these decisions are small, such as going out after work with coworkers. Others may be larger, such as purchasing a car or deciding to accept a job. Often times at work, a loving husband may say he has to check in with his wife. This shows a baseline of respect. He doesn't want to do anything that may cause her stress or more work. Inconsiderate men will either make the decision and inform their wives later, or get into an argument with them when they don't agree with their opinion.

Boyfriends, on the other hand, are less required by society to consider their girlfriend's thoughts and feelings before making a decision. However, if he seldom consults her before making choices that could impact both of them, it is a sign of things to come. The dating period is a woman's chance to evaluate a prospective life partner. If you feel like a mule during the dating period, that feeling may increase once the man feels comfortable in the security of marriage.

Now we will discuss the impact of being a professional, childless woman in the workplace. Thanks to progressive companies that have implemented more tolerant work environments for employees with children, the workplace has improved the quality of life for many employees. However, professional women with no kids may feel they have to work harder and are expected to travel and shoulder more responsibilities than women with kids. Professional women may not have daycare or babysitting concerns, but most have a household they are maintaining either fully or partially. If they are given assignments that require them to be on the road constantly, they are likely to neglect their home chores, causing more stress on the weekends while trying to play catch-up. They may also have a hard time meeting or sustaining a potential marriage partner if their singleness or childlessness causes them to get more intense assignments than other employees.

The bottom line is that all women need balance—not just women with children. A professional woman who has no kids and is single is especially vulnerable to overwork. The challenge of proving herself and being head of the household may feed a tendency to overcommit. She will have to take the responsibility of managing her time commitment to work, as well as developing an active and supportive private life.

Rita, a divorced department head and professor at a major university in the South, managed to have a balanced life. She loved her job. Because of her position and the academic topic of her department, Rita was able to meet and socialize with many interesting speakers who would come to the university. However, Rita was one of the few female members of a local scuba club. She dived all over the world and built interesting relationships outside of her job. Rita had a troubled marriage that ended in divorce, but she was able to move on and create an exhilarating second phase of her life. Though Rita didn't have any children, people would always comment that she would have made a great mother with a lot to offer a child. She chose not to have children, but at least she had a well-rounded life. She couldn't understand why other single, professional women she knew complained they couldn't meet any men. She met men constantly because she was active in a sport that was male-dominated. Rita made smart choices that allowed her to live an exciting but balanced life.

The single professional woman also needs to make sure she takes care of her health by taking time to make doctors' appointments as well as setting up annual screenings. If she allows her health needs to be neglected, she may suffer more work and personal hardships as a consequence.

According to medical studies, middle-class professional women are struck by breast cancer more than any other group. Some scientists believe the higher incidence of cancer among these women may be due to stress. One woman with a high-powered career who became a victim of breast cancer was Amy. She was a physician working in a demanding field in a young, vibrant city. She worked long hours so as not to disappoint her ever-growing circle of patients. Amy had received her annual mammograms like clockwork, but one morning when she was doing a self-examination of her breasts in the shower, she felt a lump. She scheduled an appointment with her doctor, who performed a biopsy. The results revealed Amy was stricken with a highly aggressive form of breast cancer.

Amy's doctor immediately recommended she begin chemotherapy and take time off from her job. Amy began the course of chemo but only took a week off work. She went back to seeing patients, even though she was suffering from the severe side effects of the invasive therapy. Some female family members came to help her out at home, but initially she continued to work more than she should have. The side effects became so severe Amy had to take a longer leave from her job, but she still felt guilty about it. Even though Amy had taken the Hippocratic oath as a doctor, which says you must care for those who are sick and look out for their best interests, ironically she could not do this for herself because she was too busy taking care of everyone else. Many women fall into this trap, but they need to remember that when their health goes, so does everything else. Amy was a mule to her job, and it took a major illness for her to reassess the choices she made.

In a similar situation, Karen worked under severe pressure at a demanding major company that was heavily male-dominated. Most of the male employees had stay-at-home wives who took care of the household. Karen was married, but both she and her husband worked. She became pregnant and worked through the end of her pregnancy. After her son was born, Karen felt so much pressure to return to work she only took two weeks off for maternity leave instead of the usual six weeks. She even admitted she hadn't fully healed but felt she needed to be back at work to compete. Karen continued to work like this through most of her career. She became a mule to her employer but could not see it. The one saving grace was that she had a supportive husband. He quit his job and became a househusband, providing the additional effort they needed at home. This is an example of a woman being a mule in one part of her life but a queen in another. She allowed herself to be overworked like a mule on the job, but her husband provided comfort and support at home.

How do women with no kids guarantee that friends and family treat them like queens?

- They think their spare time is just as valuable as that of someone who has kids.
- They don't let people who consciously made the decision to have kids guilt them into taking on part of their responsibility as a parent.
- They carve out time for dating and meeting potential partners.
- They don't let themselves always pull the slack for other coworkers with kids.
- They don't turn into the default babysitter for their friends who have kids.
- They don't allow themselves to be overworked at the cost of their personal development.

Women with no children often define themselves through work, and they do not have the energy-consuming challenge of raising kids. To create a well-rounded life, these women should ensure they have hobbies, friends, mates, or other activities. Shakespeare didn't say "To thine own self be true" for nothing.

Chapter 3:

Mule to the Job

The graveyards are full of indispensable men.
Charles De Gaulle

Unless we inherit great wealth, most of us need to earn a living. Over the past thirty years, women have entered the workforce in greater numbers. But, in many cases, work opportunities have not replaced the need for women to be homemakers, mothers, wives, caretakers of aging parents, or confidantes to their girlfriends. If a woman's work life is out of balance, all her other relationships will suffer, including the personal relationship she has with herself. However, the job pays the bills and allows her to live a certain lifestyle. Unfortunately, in today's world, many people become workaholics, married to their jobs. They derive their entire sense of self-worth through work. Even if you are not a workaholic, you may work for one, and his or her neurosis can easily bleed into the quality of your life.

With the popularization of technology such as cell phones, wireless access, computers, and email, many female workaholics in management positions employ state-of-the-art technology to intrude on their employees' time. Similar to a harness a mule wears, such technology enables employers to control their employees' moves during work hours and sometimes after hours. For many of today's employees, work life ends up encroaching into other areas that are critical to their lives, which we will call Critical-To-Life Areas (CTLAs). For a person to be well-rounded, he/she has to contribute some time to each of the following seven critical-to-life areas:

1. Finance
2. Work
3. Spiritual/religious beliefs
4. Family
5. Personal relationship/significant other
6. Self-improvement
7. Health

When one area, such as work, gets all the attention, the other areas suffer. Let's take a look at how this issue can manifest in a woman's life.

Marilyn was forty-one. She worked twelve-hour days for a large, well-known company. She had a top position but no subordinates to share most of her work. The following was her typical day:

5:30 – Alarm clock goes off

5:30 – 6:00 – Shower and get dressed

6:00 – 6:30 – Do hair and makeup

6:30 – 6:45 – Fix something quick to eat

6:45 – Grab the laptop she took home and jump into the car for the morning commute

6:45 – 7:30 – Drive to work

7:30 – 8:00 – Grab coffee from Starbucks, log in and check emails and voicemails

8:00 – 12:00 – Conference calls and meetings

12:00 – 12:30 – Go grab a take-out lunch

12:30 – 1:00 – Eat lunch and respond to emails that came in the morning

1:00 – 6:30 – Conference calls and meetings

6:30 – 7:30 – Drive home

7:30 – 8:00 – Pick up takeout at a restaurant in the shopping center near home

8:00 – 9:30 – Watch TV

9:30 – 10:00 – Get clothes ready for the next work day

10:00 –10:30 – Read before falling asleep

Now, this daily schedule does not account for grocery shopping, picking up dry cleaning, hair appointments, house cleaning, and miscellaneous errands. Since Marilyn is single, she has to do all these chores herself.

In the above schedule, Marilyn has very little time to cook healthy, unrushed meals. At forty-one, she does not exercise after sitting at a desk all day. She typically doesn't get together with any friends after work because she is so tired. She also hasn't had a boyfriend in ages because she never goes out to meet anyone, even on weekends. Twice a month she has to travel for business, and adding more pressure to her schedule, she is hunting down food in a strange city as well as attending business meetings out of office hours.

Is Marilyn supporting all the CTLAs equally? Well, her schedule doesn't tell us much about her finances, except she probably spends quite a bit of her disposable income on eating out. Her health is suffering because she is sedentary all day long, eats fast food, and isn't exercising. She doesn't have a significant other. She does go to church for three hours on Sunday and attends Bible study on Wednesday nights when she is in town. She talks to her mother twice a week by phone and sees her twice a year on vacation. She wants to take up a hobby, such as scuba diving, but hasn't had time to take lessons.

Clearly, Marilyn is a mule to her job. She hasn't made time to develop the other areas of her life. So, what should she do? She should set an earlier time to leave work every day to give her more quality time at home. If she left at 5:30 instead of 6:30, this would allow her to have an extra hour to herself where she could work out or prepare a meal instead of getting takeout.

She may also want to think about switching to a less demanding job within her company where she has staff who can help her do some of the work. At her current job, she is basically a one-woman show, which is not healthy for her personal life.

Oftentimes, a woman working for a workaholic manager doesn't realize she needs to have balance. His or her schedule and priorities will inevitably bleed into hers, whether she likes it or not. And even though a manager may have trouble managing his boundaries, the employees can rarely tell a manager this without seeming less committed to getting work done. Anything perceived as complaining behavior can be the kiss of death for favorable performance reviews.

Wendy was this sort of workaholic. She was a hard-charging division president. She had two sons, but they were usually with the day- or night-time nanny. The one thing Wendy was focused on was her job because she was the primary breadwinner. Her husband had a small handyman business, but didn't come close to earning Wendy's six-figure income.

Most of her employees had young children as well, but this didn't matter to Wendy. She thought meeting stretch goals was more important than getting home early to have dinner with her kids. Most of her team wanted to leave at a reasonable hour, but Wendy always kept them late in evening meetings, strategizing about the next great idea. Many complained privately to each other, but none had the guts to confront Wendy about this directly because of her tendency to berate employees in front of their peers.

Some of her employees even developed health issues related to stress, such as nervous stomachs or chronic colds. Others who could not bear the extreme work hours any longer transferred out to more balanced departments. Pride, however, made the others just stay in their positions and suffer.

Wendy's wake-up call came when she received feedback from employee surveys. Many of her employees rated her very low on work/life balance and her ability to accept ideas other than her own. Although Wendy was stunned, it didn't occur to her that she had totally ignored the pushback from the few who had been brave enough to complain and that she had intimidated others. Now that her staff had an anonymous, safe platform to express their discontent with her overbearing management style, they didn't hesitate to use it.

Management took the employee feedback seriously and transferred Wendy to another area in the business. Wendy's dismissive, uncaring behavior towards her exhausted staff was typical of many self-styled managers who derive most of their egocentric self-worth from their job. Wendy's prime motivation was to look good to her managers. Like other workaholics, Wendy secretly was a perfectionist who tried to use work to prove she was worthy of praise. She was not only a mule to work, but she was a mule to her low self-esteem, despite her apparent outward success. If she were to lose her job or become disabled, she would feel like a nobody. The work CTLA takes most of a workaholic's energy so he or she doesn't really care about other critical areas of his or her life.

Workaholics are people you see checking their Blackberrys in the movies or logging on to check email late at night, on weekends, several times a day, even while they are on vacation. They feed off the praise of their superiors and are terrified of being criticized at work. This would confirm the hidden insecurities they harbor. Are you one of these people? Are you a mule to your job?

To feel more financially secure, some people use a tool called Quicken, which helps them track expenses. It gives them a sense of where their money is being spent. You can do the same thing with your time. Get a notepad and, for a week, write down how you spend time during your day. For every hour, note where you spend your time. At the end of the week, take a look at your list of notes and do the following:

1. Come up with different categories for how you spend your time. Some examples are:
    *   Meetings (Work CTLA)
    *   Solitary project work (Work CTLA)
    *   Emails (Work CTLA)
    *   Children's activities (Family CTLA)
    *   Cooking (Health CTLA)
    *   Grooming (Self-improvement CTLA)
    *   Clothes shopping (Financial CTLA)
    *   Errands (Family CTLA)
    *   Commute time (Work CTLA)
    *   Exercise (Health CTLA)

2. Take a week's worth of time entries and allocate them to the different categories.
3. Add up the time spent in each one of the categories. What are your top three categories?
4. Now, match these categories to your Critical-To-Life Areas (CTLAs). For example, CTLA "Work" would include meeting time, email time, commute time, and solitary project work. CTLA "Health" would include exercise, cooking, and sleeping.

Ask yourself if you are happy with how you have spent most of your time over the past week. Analyze your results by answering the following questions:

- Are the seven Critical-To-Life Areas being fed?
- How many are being fed?
- Are none being fed?

The following is Marilyn's typical work-week time allocation:

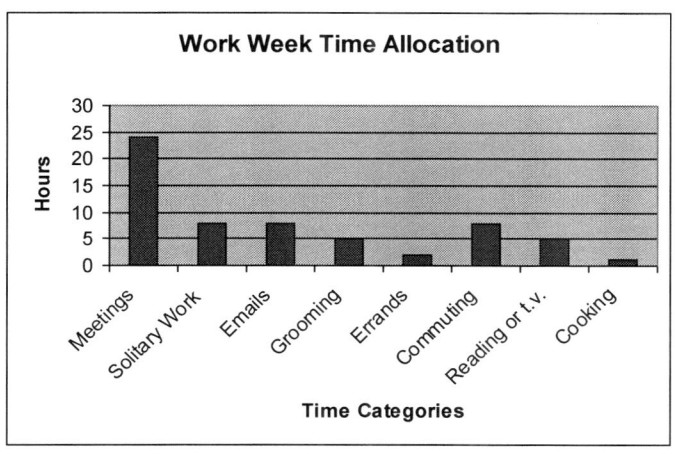

How many of her CTLAs are being met during the week? Marilyn's work CTLA is being allocated plenty of time, but her CTLAs of personal relationships, self-improvement, and health are getting virtually no time. How healthy is such a lifestyle? Most of her quality time is being spent on her career.

Generally, if less than five CTLAs are being constantly fed, you have a quality-of-life problem, and you will have to work hard to reallocate your time to ensure a healthier existence emotionally and physically. Make a note of which ones were totally neglected during the first week, and make a plan for the second week. Put time down on your calendar to spend at least one hour in each of those areas, and do the time-tracking exercise for a second week. Repeat this exercise weekly until you see an increase in the time you spend in those other CTLAs. Realistically, you may not get equal time in all areas, but you will be able to rebalance and fine-tune your schedule over the next few months to achieve a healthier, less stressful lifestyle.

Brooke recognized that her high-stress job was unhealthy. Her doctor had diagnosed her with high blood pressure and noticed her health had deteriorated. As a nurse in a very busy clinic, Brooke was so busy taking care of others she was not doing a good job of taking care of herself.

When Brooke went to her doctor for a follow-up, she was told that unless she rebalanced her life, she would develop other illnesses that would require medication. Noting the decline in her health, Brooke's doctor recommended she think about quitting or retiring. Shocked by the doctor's revelations, Brooke immediately took four days off to do some soul-searching. When she returned to work, she resigned. Now, six months later, Brooke is working far fewer hours at a new, less stressful job. She says she has never been happier and would never go back to the way things were.

In this case, Brooke's doctor was the queen because she was able to make her patient's life better mentally and physically. Without her doctor's push, Brooke would have continued to work until she dropped. Her doctor's presentation of the facts and convincing argument freed Brooke from her mule mentality and allowed her to re-structure her life.

Brooke's doctor highlights the value of having good advisors. As an adult, if you are overburdened or in a tough situation, these people may be able to do some of the thinking for you when you can't think for yourself. Sometimes people can't just count on their friends or family to give them unbiased advice that is in their best interest. If you pick well-qualified, supportive profession-als (e.g., doctors, lawyers, real estate agents, ministers, counselors, etc.) to help take care of you, they can play an invaluable role in enhancing your quality of life.

As mentioned above, a working woman needs to do her part in taking care of her personal needs. If she gets good advice from her advisors, she needs to listen. Many women are so overworked they find it hard to focus atten-tion on taking care of their needs.

How does a working woman ensure that coworkers and friends treat her like a queen?

- She doesn't miss her health appointments for work reasons.
- She doesn't talk about work constantly on weekends.

- She doesn't let work define her sense of self-importance.
- She keeps her résumé updated, just in case.
- She doesn't ever believe she is indispensable.

Technological advancements and the increase in household expenses have driven many Americans to become mules to their jobs. If you feel overwhelmed, you will have to work to rebalance your time. In some cases, this may require you to seek a less time-consuming occupation within the same company or at another company. Whatever choice you make, though, you have to remember time is like money—once it's spent, you never get it back.

Chapter 4:

Mule to the Past

Respect the past in the full measure of its desserts, but do not make the mistake of confusing it with the present nor seek in it the ideals of the future.

Jose Ingenieros

I was floored by one woman's response to my question, "What type of treatment makes you feel cared for like a queen?" She said, "I'm sorry to say I do not have that feeling. I haven't had that feeling since my husband passed away eleven years ago." I thought, "How awful! Not having the feeling of being taken care of for eleven years?" Her CTLA area of personal relationships/significant others must be getting near zero time allocation. Then I wondered, how could this be? Did she totally dedicate her life to her husband without making any substantial friendships of her own? Did she have so-called friends while he was alive who showed their true colors after his death? Did she not make enough effort to get out and establish a new social life? Like a mule, was she stubborn about changing the course of her life? Did she cling to the past?

A lot of women are raised to think that obtaining a husband, children, and a picket fence is the panacea of life. The only problem with this thinking is that most women tend to outlive men. In an article in the *Harvard Gazette* entitled "Why Women Live Longer Than Men," William Cromie reviewed data by Ruth Fretts, a Harvard obstetrician-gynecologist, and Thomas Perls, a geriatrician at Harvard Medical School. Cromie wrote:

> "In all developed countries and most undeveloped ones, women outlive men, sometimes by a margin of 10 years," Perls and Fretts note. "In the U.S., average life expectancy at birth is about 79 years for women and about 72 years for men."

So, on average, unless you marry a much younger man, you should expect to outlive your husband by seven years. This doesn't even take into account the current high statistics of divorce that ensure many contemporary women will spend some time in their life alone, even if they remarry. The woman cited spent ten years or more without anyone treating her like a queen, which highlights the fact that it is critical for women to establish a nourishing support system outside of their spouses and children. If you depend solely on your husband and children you are setting yourself up to be a mule eventually, because husbands tend to die earlier and children go off to college or move out to live their own lives. Why would a woman sabotage her happiness by putting all her eggs in one basket?

The infamous jilted wife, Betty Broderick, is a classic example of how staying a mule to your past can have disastrous results. Her husband had an affair and left her for a younger woman. Instead of mourning the loss and rebuilding her life for herself and her children, she decided to make revenge the focus of her life. She murdered him and his new wife in their new home, and was convicted of the crime. Can anyone doubt how much better her life would have been if she had moved on and found someone to love her the way she could have been loved?

I'm not advocating a woman dump her kids on the babysitter and start bar-hopping as soon as she marries and has children. However, because of kids' college transitions, husbands' shorter life spans, and the relatively high divorce rate, a woman should work hard to build strong, validating relationships with friends the same way she hopefully is planning for her retirement, though studies show some women put all their eggs in their husband's basket on this issue as well. Let's look at some examples of women who made this mistake.

Martha was married to Sam. He was a good provider but played around with other women until the day he died. Martha never bore any children, but Sam had a child out of wedlock whom he included in his will. During her marriage, Martha was the ultimate homemaker, cooking and keeping an immaculate house. When Sam died, Martha had to split some of Sam's estate with his child. She also had to depend on distant relatives to take her to the doctor and church on Sundays, since she had never learned to drive.

Inadvertently, Martha had made herself a mule to her husband. She never established friendships with people who would have cared for her when she reached those golden years.

Unlike Martha, some women who are mules in the earlier part of their lives due to poor decision-making eventually wise up later in life. Jane is an example of this type of woman. She fell for Felix, who was extremely good-looking but considered Jane to be below his social class. They went out and eventually made a physical connection, and Jane bore two children by Felix, one year apart. Since Felix considered Jane below his social class, he never offered to marry her. When Felix finally went off into the sunset, Jane became a mule because she had to care for two children alone, without any education to fall back on. This, in turn, made her aging parents mules because they had to help care for the kids when Jane went off to work her minimum-wage job. In the early part of her life, Jane's key CTLAs were work and family.

Jane did the best she could to raise the two children, and eventually they went off to college. She never gave up her dreams—she took music lessons, finished her high school degree, attended church regularly, and moved to a busier city, since she was still a fairly young woman. She met and fell in love with a good man from church who worshipped her. She also made great friends, and these friends visited her when she was sick from diabetes or had worked herself a little too hard helping to plan local parties. Later in life, Jane increased her focus on the CTLA of personal relationships/significant other. Jane learned from the pain inflicted by poor decision-making and made the migration from "mule" to "queen" status with smarter relationship choices later in life.

Ironically, some women are mules to the happiness they felt as a child, and they never do the things they should to ensure adult happiness. They may have been "Daddy's girls" whose needs were catered for by hardworking fathers who wanted their daughters to have a better life than they'd had as kids. Unfortunately, this special treatment can lead women to feel a sense of entitlement or a need to be the center of attention. This may be acceptable behavior for a child who has a doting parent, but this same behavior carried into adulthood can make it hard for an individual to maintain healthy relationships with other adults.

Some women may expect men to spoil them with attention and gifts like their fathers did. They experience disappointment when today's working boyfriend or spouse can't fill Daddy's shoes. These women may even acknowledge that they are slightly spoiled. Some mask this as having "high expectations," which, in reality, no adult can fill. However, they don't just exhibit this entitlement with their significant other. Their demands spill over into their friendships and work relationships as well. This can be a real nightmare for people who have to set realistic expectations with these women who are still emotional mules to their childhood. Many of these women may float from job to job or friend to friend looking for that special treatment they think they deserve.

Another factor that leads women to become mules stems from their upbringing. In many households, one parent is more present than the other. The other parent may be absent due to divorce, working two jobs, working remotely, or staying away from home to avoid a difficult spouse. Sometimes, the parent that spends more time at home may have issues such as alcoholism, drug use, depression, and so on. This is a very difficult environment for a child to grow up in. There can be abuse (mental or physical) or neglect that can negatively impact a child. As shown in many psychological studies, some children repeat this behavior while some go on to lead much healthier lives, selecting nurturing adult relationships.

Michelle was a woman who decided not to be a mule to her past. Her father, a high-ranking military officer, was deployed overseas. Her mother stayed in the United States with the kids. The loneliness and pressure eventually got to Michelle's mother. She became addicted to drugs and started seeing other men. Michelle and her brothers found themselves alone or staying at a relative's home a lot of time. The father was a loving man but had to earn a living for his family and honor his military commitment. He came to see his children whenever he was on leave and brought them to see him whenever he could. The continuous reinforcement of his love and support through frequent phone calls and visits did foster some feeling of being cared for in Michelle and her brothers.

Michelle, as the oldest, had to step up sometimes in her father's absence to take care of her brothers. After doing well in school despite her mother's issues, she was accepted into college on an athletic scholarship. After graduation, she went on to establish a thriving career in a helping profession. She also married and established a stable family for her own kids. Her family is now the nucleus of strength for her larger family. When she and her husband get tied up with a business meeting, her brothers take care of her kids, and she does the same for them when necessary. Michelle made wise choices as a young adult that didn't force her to remain a mule to her childhood. Her CTLA of family gets plenty of time allocation even though she invests a good amount of time in her CTLA area of work/career. Though she has a job, Michelle is able to spend a lot of quality time with her husband and children as well. They adore and respect her as a mother and a wife. She has become the "queen" of her primary and extended family.

How does a queen continuously grow?

- She doesn't talk about how great she was in the past.
- She is always willing to try new things.
- She travels to broaden her exposure.
- She learns from her parents' mistakes and doesn't repeat them.
- She doesn't carry "Daddy's girl" tendencies into her adult relationships with men.

Staying a mule to your past allows you to be beaten twice—once by a situation that was not under your control, and then again by poor choices you make as an adult that can put you into an overburdened situation. Many young adults struggle with how to move past a negative upbringing to a happier, more supported adulthood. Individual therapy and support groups, such as Al-Anon and ACA, provide a much-needed starting point for many adults to prevent themselves from enacting oppressive patterns as adults. To get recommendations on effective support groups and counselors, you can speak with your physician or others you know who have overcome past patterns through therapy. The beauty of being an adult is that you have choices about what your life will look and feel like. Making choices that honor your time and your worth put you closer and closer to having the nurtured adult life you deserve.

Chapter 5:

Mule to Popular Opinion

Anybody who is any good is different from anybody else.

Felix Frankfurter

"Competitiveness" is a word familiar to most men and women. Healthy competition between individuals can be a good thing because it motivates people to go beyond their personal goals and achieve something even greater. However, there can be a downside if competition with one's peers is taken too far.

Women often talk among themselves about how competitive other women are. The competition can be as simple as who has the cutest or most successful husband, who dresses better, who is skinnier, who has a more successful career, or whose kids are smarter or more popular. Women who get caught up in popular opinions about what is "better" can be setting themselves up for a tiring run on an unending treadmill, always chasing the next hot thing. Just like a mule that performs to be rewarded with food, these women alter their behavior to get validation from their friends or family. These women are never comfort-able with themselves because their self-esteem is riddled with insecurity. This leads to some passive-aggressive behaviors, such as backstabbing, blaming, whining, and ridiculous spending, to keep up with peers.

In any culture that has queens, the queens don't seem to compete with anybody. They are confident in them-selves and deal with others in a very calm, wise manner. An image of a queen who is neurotic and jealous is not one you will see often. Queen Elizabeth I was often told that a woman could not lead. Rather than feeling anxious and bowing to popular thought, she pulled it together and became one of the world's most effective rulers. Queen Elizabeth II has ruled for over fifty years. Whenever there is turmoil in the Royal Family, the citizens of Great Britain look to her for reaction and calm. She is widely respected as the ultimate authority when it comes to British rule.

Some women abandon their truest beliefs for the sake of others, and it is amazing how much value some women place in their family's opinion when it comes to picking a suitor. Sharon was one of those women who prized her mother's opinion. Sharon was studying to be a psychia-trist and was nearing the end of her studies at a prestigious medical school. Her mother would get her hair done at a popular beauty salon in a medium-sized town. The owner of the beauty salon had a handsome son who was studying to be an actor, and she wanted to fix him up with Sharon. Sharon knew the young man and thought he was cute and nice. However, Sharon's mother told her he was just an actor and she shouldn't be bothered with him since his career was not as influential as Sharon's. Sharon listened to her mother and decided to decline his mother's urgings for the two to meet. The son of the beauty salon owner went on to become one of the most successful actors of all time. His current wife lives in luxury in Beverly Hills and New York and is well known for her own talents and charity work. Her husband always comments on how she stuck with him since his earliest days as a struggling actor. Whenever he speaks about her in public, he heaps praise on her for how supportive she has always been. Sharon, to this day, still regrets not following her own mind and going out with the beautician's son. She had been a mule to her mother's opinion and society's view of the young man's profession as well.

Gloria Steinem is a renowned female activist. She is also very smart and beautiful; in fact, she did a stint as a Playboy Bunny and went on to cofound *Ms. Magazine*. Steinem was often criticized for pursuing her career instead of settling down with a nice husband. She lived her life on her own terms and impacted many women's minds in a positive way. She married in her own time and not according to everyone else's opinion. She became very happily married late in life. She could have yielded to popular pressure, but she had the wisdom at an early age to live her life the way she saw fit, and she has had a richer life as a result.

Many successful people have said that to be good at something, you have to really have a passion for it. Some women haven't identified their personal passion and may mirror the behaviors or choices of their friends or families. There are some very obvious examples of this mimicking that have life-altering effects.

Picking a life partner is one of the most important decisions a woman can make. If she makes a poor choice, a woman could, at best, end up in a dull marriage—at worst, in an abusive one. Impulsive women looking for validation may decide to marry when a sister or close friend marries. Hidden competitiveness may surface, making the single female feel that her sister or friend is moving on in their life while she is being left behind.

Anna, a successful professional, saw her sister planning a big elaborate wedding. Anna had been separated and living with a guy for four years, and she seemed perfectly happy. Neither she nor her boyfriend had finalized their divorces due to the legal expenses involved. When her sister Jody became engaged and set a spring wedding date, however, Anna felt outdone. She pressured her boyfriend to finalize his divorce and even paid for the legal fees associated with filing the paperwork. Anna then chased down her husband, who was living in another city, to get him to sign documents she had asked her divorce attorney to draw up. This was all done in a rush to enable her to set a wedding date before her sister's.

Why would someone go through these extremes to marry first? Simple. Anna was a mule to others' perceptions of her. She couldn't merely be shacking with a guy when her sister was having a big wedding with all the trappings. However, the root cause lay in the fact that Anna was insecure and needed validation from others. She couldn't live her own life on her own timeline. She was a mule to her family's perception of her.

Like some older women who look to their friends for cues on when to marry, teenage girls may be influenced by their friends in deciding to have a baby. In the eighties and nineties, there was a huge spike in the number of teenage pregnancies in the US. Many middle-class voters and politicians criticized the huge amount of money that went to subsidizing the lifestyles of teen mothers. Some government studies were instigated to look into the reasons these young girls would make the life-changing decision to become a mother without the support of a partner. One of the reasons may have been that their friends were having children. In a study of the health-care industry, "Teenage Motherhood: Its Relationship to Undetected Learning Problems," the author, Helen Rauch-Elnekave, looks for the root causes of teenage mothers deciding to have a baby. She examines the possibility that these groups of girls may have learning problems. In her study, however, "three out of four had one or more friends who were pregnant or had already given birth, while 38 percent said they had four or more friends who were pregnant or already parenting." These findings may indicate that even at this young age, these women were mules to popular opinion, which in this case held that it is fine to have a baby as a teenage, single mother.

How does a queen make decisions?

- She consults others, but the final choice is hers.
- She doesn't always care what others think.
- She takes unpopular, but morally correct stances.
- She participates in at least one activity that is different from her friends.

As evidenced above, basing one's decisions on popular opinion can have a detrimental impact on one's life. This extreme validation behavior occurs among women in lower income groups as well as educated, professional women. But most would agree the impact is far worse on poor women with few options for economic betterment. Unfortunately, when these decisions to fit in finally have consequences, the very people they were trying to impress are usually not there to bail them out of their self-imposed misery. A woman has to do some self-examination and ask, "Why am I really choosing to do this?" If she does not, she will go through life backing herself into a dark corner by making one bad decision after another.

Chapter 6:

Adult Mule to Family of Origin

I think the family is the place where the most ridiculous and least respectable things in the world go on.
Ugo Betti

Southerners are known for being family oriented. They often have large, extended families with whom they socialize. This is great if everybody's individual rights are respected; however, sometimes there is a dark side to all of this closeness. Many senior family members may feel they have the right to control a family member's decisions right into adulthood. Everybody needs wise counsel, but everybody should also have the right to develop her or his own life without interference.

Historically, in the South, there were less urban areas where young adults could work and meet transferees or professionals from other areas who had relocated for opportunity. Young women may have dated, married, and lived in the same small towns they grew up in. Many depended on their family of origin for activities. This fostered the continuation of close relationships of children with parents and siblings well into adulthood. However, education and the growth of the New South have allowed these young southerners to work and socialize with transplants from all over the world. Cities such as Atlanta, Birmingham, Charlotte, Raleigh, and Nashville are shining examples of the cosmopolitan New South.

Nonetheless, a woman who grew up in the South, went to college, and settled in or near the area in which she grew up may still struggle to have an independent life. Sometimes, her parents, who may be retired, may not have many exciting things happening in their lives. They may meddle in their grown children's lives in order to feel a sense of purpose. This interference may impede the growth and development of an adult woman. If she fights the interference, it is likely to cause a family power struggle. This conflict may be tough to handle if she also has a stressful job in a competitive work environment. Some adult women do a good job establishing boundaries, thereby controlling their family of origin's involvement. Some women are not so strong and begin to cave in under the unfair pressure. A mule is a hybrid breed between a horse and a donkey. Women who are mules to their family of origin are hybrids that operate between childhood and adulthood, unable to enforce grown-up boundaries due to their dependence on the approval of family.

Christie was one of those women smothered by family demands. She lived fifty miles from the rural community where her parents and older sibling lived. She had moved to a larger city for better job opportunities where modern-day conveniences were available within the neighborhood. Through her job and new church, she established her own friendships and activities. Her older sister, who still lived on the farm, would solicit family members to pressure

Christie to drive the fifty miles to attend the family church when they were having special functions, which seemed to be every other week.

As a manager, Christie was responsible for a large staff and visible deliverables to clients. She worked a lot of overtime to get her job done and still had to make time for her husband and household chores. The pressure from her older sister caused her to make an effort to drive to her hometown church for some functions even though she was tired, but what Christie began to see was that no matter how many functions she drove to at her childhood church, it was never enough to please her sister or family. Clearly, Christie's sister had made a mule of her. She felt tired on Monday mornings after making the long drives Sundays to go to her home church. Many things remained undone at home because Christie didn't have as much time on the weekends to take care of household tasks. She soon realized she had to live her own life or would be broken down by the stress of trying to please everyone in her life. She told her family directly that she couldn't continue to drive to their church functions, and instead, she decided to get more involved in a church around the corner.

Christie refused to allow her guilt-inducing family to turn her into a mule. This caused her to have a better quality of life with her husband and allowed her to deepen her new friendships. Her change in attitude helped her focus on other CTLAs, such as her significant other, friends, and health.

Women from oppressed cultures may also have this problem. These groups sometimes feel isolated or rejected by society. Family members may be stuck in the past on a memory of how they were painfully rejected when they tried to assimilate into a larger culture. They may project this bitterness on their children without even realizing it.

Gloria was the daughter of a Cuban-American immigrant family. She was very smart and always did well in school. Her father was very loving and worked two jobs to support the family. Her mother Alice worked as a teacher at the local community college. Alice always told her daughter that education was the most surefire way to a successful career and life. She constantly told Gloria that Cuban girls had to work twice as hard to get ahead. She warned Gloria that young Cuban boys were dangerous and just wanted one thing. She also told Gloria men didn't want ready-made families and that if she had a child out of wedlock, no successful Cuban man would want her.

Gloria's mother constantly criticized Gloria's father by saying he didn't make enough money and hadn't furthered his education. Alice felt she deserved a more articulate partner who could provide them with a better standard of living. Gloria's parents frequently argued over money, and the household in which she grew up was full of strife.

When Gloria finally went off to college, she felt free. Her mother continued to call and put pressure on her about keeping her grades up, and she needled Gloria about how much money she was spending as a student. Gloria continued to study but felt something was missing from her life. Then, one night when she went to a party with some friends at a military base, she met Carlos. Carlos seemed fun and confident, which was the opposite of how Gloria felt. She began seeing Carlos, and soon became pregnant.

Gloria told Carlos about the pregnancy. She became scared when he started distancing himself, saying he already had a child he was supporting financially. Gloria felt alone, and turned to her parents for help. She secretly wanted to keep her baby and hoped her parents would help her. Unfortunately, Gloria's mother went ballistic. She told Gloria that having this baby would ruin her future. She said Gloria would end up like all of the other poor Cuban girls in the city. She said that even if she were to finish college, no one would hire a single Cuban girl with a baby as a professional in a big corporation. Gloria ultimately caved in to the pressure and had an abortion. She felt she didn't have a choice since no one was supporting her.

Eventually, Gloria did go on to finish her studies and get a professional job. Her mother bragged to all of her friends about what great money Gloria was making as an accountant. Gloria was proud of her accomplishments but always regretted the fact that she had not kept her baby. She resented yielding to her mother's pressure about raising a child alone. As an adult, Gloria made it a priority to build a new life and distance herself from her fearful family. She felt she had been a mule to her mother's insecurity and status-consciousness, and she felt she had paid a high price. Everything had revolved around making her culture proud, as opposed to making decisions based on how the issues affected her individual life. Even though her parents lived according to the values of their culture, she didn't want to. She took a new job in California and began making friends outside of her Cuban-American community. She wanted different perspectives around her, not just one. She was beginning to focus on the CTLAs of self-improvement and spiritual freedom, instead of just family. She knew she didn't want what she had grown up around—fear and pressure.

How does a queen establish her own life apart from her family's influence?

- She marries whomever she wants.
- She has children when she wants.
- She lives where she wants.
- She realizes her parents have the freedom to make their own mistakes and that she should also have that same privilege.

Gloria exercised her choice to live her own life as an adult. Like most people, she will make mistakes, but they will be her mistakes, not those imposed on her by her family. As a child you are dependant on your parents, but as an adult you have the authority to make decisions to facilitate your own happiness. Others have been allowed to live their lives on their own terms; you have a right to live your life according to yours.

Chapter 7:

Mule to Listening

The first duty of love is to listen.

Paul Tillich

Time is the most important capital you have. Most people can earn more money, but they cannot recover lost time. We make decisions on how to spend our time every day. We spend some at work to support ourselves; we spend some with our families; we spend some with our friends, hoping the time invested will be equally rewarding for us as it is for them.

With the advent of modern technology, however, many of us feel we have less time than ever before. Personal Blackberrys, work Blackberrys, cell phones, wireless cards, portable laptops, and text messages all place more constraints on our time than technology did twenty or thirty years ago. Some folks using all these modern-day conveniences have to work harder than those in the past due to their entanglement with these electronic leashes.

Many folks who are older or ill wish they could retrieve some of the time they may have wasted on unfulfilling choices. How you spend your spare time outside of work says a lot about who you are. How you let people dominate your time also says a lot about your boundaries. Just like any other resource, people who have little consideration for your needs can drain your resources. Many women have a relative or friend who goes on and on about his or her problems, oblivious to the fact their listener may have other plans for the day. If you find yourself doing way more listening than talking to people in your personal life, you may unknowingly have become a mule to listening to others more than they are willing to listen to you.

One easy way to gauge this is to make a note of how many times, when you are talking to a sister, friend, or other acquaintance, they go on and on about something that is important to them without asking how you are doing. If you could lay the phone down for two minutes, pick it up, and still hear them going on and on, then you have a problem. The need some people have to monopolize the conversation is clearly a sign of self-absorption and disrespect. It is almost as if by ignoring your needs they are saying their lives are more important. Manipulators control a woman's time by first soliciting her pity. Then the manipulator goes on to dominate the conversation while the listener's time is swindled away. To have a quality friendship, all parties' needs have to be considered and addressed, not just those of one person.

One woman who needed to set boundaries was Kelly. She was a pleasant, upbeat person most of the time. However, when her sister Ada called, Kelly would get irritated and depressed. Ada would call and immediately launch into a stressful work-related or family issue without even asking Kelly a basic, sincere question about how her day was going. Sometimes, Kelly would have to interrupt Ada to let the kids in from school, but Ada would talk so fast and loud that she wouldn't even hear Kelly gently trying to interrupt her. In fact, Kelly sometimes even had to shout into the phone to get Ada's attention.

Eventually, Kelly stood up for herself on the phone and told Ada she felt overburdened by people calling to dump their problems on her. Ada didn't like hearing this but began to change her behavior in order to accommodate Kelly. Fortunately, Kelly stood up for her rights as a sister and didn't let Ada use up her time indiscriminately.

Another way to gauge how open your friends and family are to listening is to see how long they give you the floor when you are talking. If they find a way to interrupt you whenever you are talking and take the story back to them, then you also have an unfair listening situation where your needs aren't being met.

When people interrupt you, they are showing that what they have to say is more important than what you are saying. Even worse, they might not have been listening to you at all, because they are tired of hearing you talk, and interrupt you to talk about what they think is more important—themselves.

Allison and Daisy had known each other for fifteen years. People often called Daisy because she was a nonjudgmental listener. Daisy held a religious belief that was open and welcoming. Others felt this loving, spiritual connection, which led to many incoming calls, day and night. Her acquaintances could open up about their problems and feel heard. Her friend Allison also had great listening and advising skills, and many people called to talk to her as well.

Ironically, though, a problem occurred when Allison and Daisy talked to each other on the phone. Daisy had been so used to listening to other people without anyone really listening to her. When she talked to Allison, Daisy would interrupt her and start talking about an unrelated topic, such as her boyfriend or economic woes. Allison tolerated this for a while because she really liked Daisy. Eventually, after wondering why Allison had abruptly hung up, Daisy realized she had been dominating the conversation and called back later to apologize. At first, the apologies made Allison feel better, because she felt Daisy was truly sorry for her insensitive behavior. However, when Allison would start talking to Daisy within a period of a couple of weeks, Daisy would slip back into the same old habit.

Allison slowly began to disengage from Daisy because she felt her listening needs were not being met. Allison felt used and unimportant, and realized she spent too much time listening to people and not receiving. She had become a mule to her so-called friends. She decided to redraw the boundaries and began a program of self-care.

Allison developed a new health-care regime. She converted the time she usually spent listening to friends in the morning on her way to work into time for improving her health. She made exercising early in the morning before work her priority and began losing weight. This was great self-care for Allison because it helped reduce her blood pressure and weight. She was able to feel better and fit into clothes she hadn't been able to wear for years.

Did Allison feel guilty about her newly imposed boundaries? No. She realized others weren't concerned about taking care of her needs. They were interested only in their needs being met. Allison focused on feeding the friendships she had neglected by spending too much time listening to parasites who had no regard for her time or feelings. These reinvigorated friendships gave her a platform for discussing her issues as well as exploring new ideas for projects.

The only regret Allison had was that she hadn't redrawn her boundaries sooner. She felt sad when she thought back on all the times she had needed to be heard but let these "friends" ignore what she was saying. Now, one of the criteria for investing in a new relationship was that the person needed to seem interested in what was happening in her life.

There is another aspect to consider when you are talking to someone who is doing most of the talking. Perhaps you feel the person you are talking to would not provide a safe, non-judgmental place where you could open up. This may cause you to say little and get caught in the listening trap. Why invest time in someone who feels comfortable opening up to you but doesn't reciprocate by making you comfortable in expressing your real feelings to them? It's a one-sided friendship that's unhealthy and turns you into a mule for a selfish talker who is cornering your time.

A common one-sided relationship is that between siblings. Cameron and Mary were sisters. Cameron was single and Mary was married. Cameron was a working professional who had an active social life. She would go out on dates and have dinner and drinks with her friends after work. Sometimes, when Cameron would meet a new guy she felt had a lot of potential, she would mention her interest to Mary and briefly describe the guy. Mary would listen intently and make comments.

Cameron started noticing a pattern, though. After listing to Cameron talk about a guy, Mary would make comments that focused on unknown or potentially negative aspects about him. For example, Cameron told Mary she had met a really nice cop, and Mary made comments like "Cops are crazy" or "Cops cheat really badly" or "He might be a dirty cop." Cameron had barely told her anything about the guy, but Mary still started expounding on negative stereotypes to cast doubt in Mary's mind.

Mary's critical comments weren't just limited to Cameron's potential suitors. Mary would also talk about any new female friends Cameron had met and enjoyed socializing with. For example, Cameron met Lana at work. Lana was outgoing and gregarious and seemed like a nice person. When Cameron told Mary about Lana, Mary immediately launched into how dangerous it was to socialize with people from work. Mary also said that Lana's gregariousness might damage Cameron's reputation since Cameron was quiet and very private.

Furthermore, whenever Mary would mention something about her husband not taking responsibility for important things, Cameron would offer heartfelt suggestions, advice, or constructive criticism. Mary would immediately jump to her husband's defense, even though she was the one who had brought up the issue in the first place. Basically, Mary wanted to talk about her husband's problems but didn't want any commentary back from her sister. Cameron and Mary's conversations and relationship were one-sided.

When Cameron realized Mary may have been trying to sabotage her social life, she became very cautious about what she shared with Mary. This caused a phenomenon Cameron could not have predicted. Mary gladly filled the empty space in the conversation that had been left by Cameron's lack of disclosure. Mary would go on and on about every aspect of her life, while Cameron became a prisoner to Mary's endless stories. In other words, Mary had subconsciously tried to control Cameron by criticizing her judgment in selecting personal relationships. Now that Cameron wasn't commenting much, Mary began to monopolize the conversation and control her time.

Cameron realized Mary had turned her into a mule and decided to limit her phone interactions with Mary, except on family issues. Cameron worked extra hard to establish supportive external friendships so she wasn't so dependant on Mary's feedback. Cameron's new friends were more optimistic and objective. They gave her hope and constructive criticism when she needed it. Cameron escaped the mule trap Mary had laid for her and found other friends who were more supportive. Ironically, her dating life picked up, and currently she is happy in a relationship with a kind, supportive man.

A woman may convince herself that maybe it's not important that relationships consist of two people who listen to each other. She may think, "If a person talks to me, that person must care about me." This is not necessarily true, though. People interact in a lot of ways, but establishing a rapport doesn't necessarily mean they are considerate. People get anxious when they don't have paper towels to wipe their hands, for example, but when they do have a paper towel, they quickly wipe their hands and discard it. Don't be anybody's paper towel. Make them respect and meet your need to be heard.

Time is a precious thing. When you offer to spend time with someone, it is a gift that should be appreciated. If those you deal with take your time for granted, then you have a real problem in terms of how you are being treated. The time you spend with unappreciative, selfish people could be used for your own self-improvement. Instead of wasting your valuable time with parasites who are sucking the emotional joy out of you, you could be exercising, reading, cooking, or working on a hobby you love.

How does a queen listen to her friends?

- She doesn't let others monopolize her time with their problems.
- She picks friends who will listen to her like she listens to them.
- She doesn't interrupt when she is listening to others.
- She doesn't give one-word, short answers when asked a question.
- She doesn't watch TV or surf the Internet while she talks to you.

People who are inconsiderate of your time are typically very self-absorbed people. If something happens and you really need them, they would always have a more important commitment to explain why they couldn't help you or don't have the time. Having supportive friends is one of the greatest treasures in life. They allow you to focus on your CTLA of self-improvement while helping them improve as well.

When your children grow up and leave home, when you get divorced, or when your parents die, good friends will be with you. As with the stock market, you have to invest in friendships that will reward you over time with hours of pleasurable companionship. If you realize some-one you have spent time listening to is sabotaging you or is focused on herself or himself, move on to the next stock.

Chapter 8:

Mule to Organizations

You cannot be really first-rate at your work if your work is all you are.

Anna Quindlen

Many of today's women participate in extracurricular organizations. Society looks favorably on the many people who volunteer, those who give their time to their church, social service groups, professional organizations, and charities. A common problem with some of these groups is that they don't work hard enough to recruit volunteers to lessen the workload on those who do. Many have a few people doing most of the work. For those who volunteer, this consumes a lot of their time and increases the risk of burnout. Church functions are among the activities that can lead members to burn out.

Some women have the gift of being great organizers. They can assemble, motivate, and establish activities that accomplish goals and address charitable needs. What can sometimes happen in these groups is that the members do very little while the organizer does almost everything.

Whenever the organization reaches out for volunteers, people are either too busy or lazy to step up. Some women, just like mules, are very dutiful, but show little consideration for their own need for rest. This can cause women who start out with good intentions and plenty of energy to work themselves into a state of exhaustion.

Freda is an example of an overworked woman in the church. She worked in a professional environment for years, learning very good organizational and project- management skills. The church meetings she attended were becoming chaotic, so she would step in to put structure around the process to help meet the group's objectives.

Freda's church had meetings several nights a week. As the word got out about Freda's great organizing ability, more and more of the church's groups would ask her to coordinate. Before long, Freda was spending most nights at church, while none of the members were being cross-trained to take over some of her duties. Her phone began ringing late into the night, even if she had just gotten home from a church meeting.

Things really became unbearable when members started asking Freda to help them organize their personal projects outside the church too. Freda's husband complained that though she was trying to serve God, the church members were using her. To her husband, Freda acknowledged the fatigue and burnout she was feeling. She decided to cut back on all but one of the groups at the church. To relieve pressure on herself, Freda began referring members to professional services that could help with their personal problems.

Many people seek spiritual nourishing at the end of their long workweek. There's a current trend where some professionals are so busy and burnt out by Sunday they prefer to watch ministers preach the message on television. They feel they can get a spiritual message without driving or being pressured to volunteer for additional missions at church. One minister who has drawn a large home-viewing congregation is Joel Osteen.

Joel Osteen has a large viewership and fills a void in a lot of people's lives. Many folks are surrounded by people who take without giving verbal encouragement, and that is why his following is so large and diverse. A lot of people in today's world are hurting because they have no one to care for them emotionally, physically, or financially. His word on Sunday may be the only time they hear someone rooting for them all week. While some other high-profile ministers seem judgmental and punitive, Osteen comes across as being concerned, relating the lessons in the Bible to their contemporary problems.

The Bible instructs believers to cultivate fellowship. Mingling with other believers is a great way to have human contact in a very cold, isolating world. However, the Bible says nothing about letting people use you up without considering your feelings. Women, in particular, need to be careful of their time and set appropriate boundaries with other church members so the church's progress does not rest solely on the backs of a few members.

Other groups that can drain precious time if not managed properly include professional organizations, alumni chapters of sororities and fraternities, and some charitable groups.

Vicky loved her sorority. The group had provided her with many good times in college. She had fond memories of her involvement in the group's community service projects. She also became active in the local alumni chapter when she relocated to a new city in the Northeast for her job. The alumni group planned social events and scholarship fundraisers, and Vicky was right in the midst of the planning.

She began to notice that when meetings were planned, she was assigned to take minutes and follow up on the action items from the sessions. Other members came up with great ideas for functions but didn't want to dirty their hands with their execution. Vicky had a strong public relations background from her day job, and the group leveraged her skills heavily. Instead of feeling invigorated when she left these sessions, she felt drained. She would stop and get fast food dinners. After arriving home, she would slump down in front of the television. This behavior lasted several months, causing her gym shoes to collect dust and her weight to skyrocket.

Vicky had hoped to meet some grad members of the brother fraternity that was also helping, but the only men she ever met were fraternity brothers who were married or engaged. Being involved with the group allowed her to meet some female acquaintances but no real close friends. She realized the sorority leaders and their activities were draining her time and energy and offered little in return. For months, they had been making a mule of her, and she was tired of it. She decided to quit the group and join a jogging group in her neighborhood to revitalize her health routine. She still attends some of the sorority parties occasionally but is glad to be a guest rather than a coordinator.

Social groups are fine as long as the volunteer workload is balanced. If a few members are planning everything, then the group is not well managed and it's time to move on.

Ironically, professional organizations can also be afflicted by parasites who drain your time and energy. Erica joined her local engineering professional organization. They scheduled meetings for an hour on a weeknight, but these usually exceeded two hours because some members would ramble on and on while the moderator just sat there. When Erica would try to bring some of the speakers back to the topic, they became irritated with her for interrupting their monologue. She decided to try another group she had heard about in a nearby city. She liked the fact that their membership was diverse—black and white men and women, married and single. They started meetings on time and got out on time because some of the members had families to go home to. Even though going to the new professional group's meetings meant a slightly longer drive, she still got home earlier after meetings.

A subconscious reason why some women overcommit to a volunteer organization may be that they are trying to run from other areas of their lives that may be unpleasant. Kiera was one of these women. She was married with two kids, but her husband, Mike, had a high-profile job that required him to travel five days a week. She was at home with the kids, constantly shuttling them from one activity to another. Mike came home on Fridays. Kiera was more than happy to dump the kids on him on Fridays so she could attend the local PTA meetings. Kiera freely volunteered to organize any activities the PTA planned.

She often said she wanted to improve the school's environment for her kids, but deep down, she wanted to keep herself busy enough to avoid the loneliness she felt during Mike's absences. Since he had been gone so much, she didn't feel that close to him. She felt like his returns threw the whole family's routine off balance. She would resent having to have sex with this "stranger" whenever he came home. Busying herself with the PTA was a way to focus on something else. Kiera got a sense of purpose from being the lead organizer for PTA functions. With her husband, though, she always felt like a supporting player. Her life had not turned out the way she had envisioned it, and the PTA provided a constant diversion.

If a woman is too involved with a volunteer organization, it may reveal that she is running from some emptiness in her life. As with any other quick fix, the void will still be there and may grow over time. A woman needs to ask, "Why do I spend so much time volunteering with a group? Am I spending more time than anyone else?" The best thing may be to take a break or essentially enact a "fast" from the organization to get in touch with the source of the discomfort she is really feeling. A woman shouldn't squander her time by simply keeping busy. By being over-involved, she may be feeding the CTLA of personal relationships, but she is most likely neglecting the CTLAs of self-improvement and health. She should honor her life by rebalancing her time as well as acknowledging and fixing any emptiness that makes her vulnerable to overextending herself.

How does a queen allocate some of her time to organizations?

- She helps out some but doesn't let them become solely dependant on her efforts.
- She doesn't let them guilt her into coming to meetings when she is tired.
- She doesn't let them take more than a couple hours a week, if she works.
- She doesn't always volunteer.

It is important for a woman to balance her extracurricular activities. These allow her to network, meet new people who may become friends, and learn about what is going on in the world outside of work. But as with a day job, involvement in these groups should not be entirely selfless. It should also be fun and rewarding. If that is not the case, a woman needs to reassess whether involvement in an organization is right for her.

Chapter 9:

Mule to Victorian Ideals

The man who views the world at fifty the same way as
he did at twenty has wasted thirty years of his life.

Muhammad Ali

Even though the women's movement has instigated
a lot of progress in the hiring, promotion, and pay of
women, socially speaking, many women are still living
in the Victorian age. Unfortunately, women have been so-
cialized by semi-Victorian mothers to look attractive, put
themselves out on display as if they were a piece of fruit
on a cart, and let a man pick them. These ideals are out-
dated since they don't take advantage of the new access
women have to men in the workplace, gyms, professional
organizations, and so on. Shockingly, many professional
women still believe, even after forty, that a man will see
them, ask them out, date them, and propose to them—
all without them going any place other than work and
church. Like a mule, they repeatedly follow the course
set by someone else, never questioning whether the ideals
are outdated.

Since fewer men are going to college every year, there are fewer single men in the workplace. Many who are may have married right out of college. It's still possible for a woman to meet an available man at work, but the pickings are slimmer. What would help her is to get out and join clubs and organizations where men gather. Doing the work–home–church cycle just won't cut it.

Lindsey was a well-paid professional woman who worked in a marketing group with a large company based in the Midwest. She was a very stylish dresser and was considered attractive. She was also single and hadn't had a real date for over two years. At work, she was assigned to one hot project after another. This fed her ego and paycheck, but it did very little for her social life since she worked a lot of overtime.

Lindsey's routine became work, home, and shopping on the weekends, and church on Sunday. This routine went on for weeks, months, years, and she often wondered why she couldn't meet any men. She had hoped to meet some in church, but it seemed many guys her age weren't attending Sunday services unless they attended with their wife and kids. She didn't know what else to do because she had been raised by a Southern, conservative mother who had married and had several kids. Her mother could only teach her what had worked for her. After picking up a take-out dinner, she would often spend at least an hour each night talking to her mother on the phone before going to bed, and Lindsey wasn't meeting people. Her CTLA of finding a significant other was nonexistent and was not being allocated any quality time.

Lindsey began to realize her mother couldn't give her great advice about how to meet someone. She resorted to another semi-Victorian idea of asking married couples to fix her up with someone. This sometimes works; for example, John and Jackie Kennedy met through the introduction of a friend. But, more often than not, married couples usually socialize with married couples and know very few single, available men. Also, since they are not out in the hunt themselves, they may not look as hard at the person as you would if you were doing the screening yourself. It's like a retired athlete helping a team screen for talent, versus an athlete who's currently playing on the team. Their assessment skills may not be as sharp.

Lindsey met a couple of guys this way, but they always seemed to have something wrong with them that her married friends had missed during the screening process.

Lindsey also participated in some social activities with her group of girlfriends. The only problem with this was that they were all looking too. When they were out together they could be intimidating for a guy to approach, even if he liked one of them. Although this behavior has been ineffective, Lindsey continues to do it.

How should Lindsey modify her behavior to meet prospective boyfriends? She should start by taking up one activity in which she has even the slightest interest, which would allow her to get out of the house and meet new people. She currently invests so much time talking to her mother and her gaggle of girlfriends that she is not making way for anybody new to come into her life.

Another Victorian idea that many women still hold onto is the tendency to date only people within their own culture. Most people feel a familiarity with others who look like them and who were raised with the same cultural beliefs. This is fine if there are plenty of available men in your own culture, regardless of the age bracket you find yourself in. However, if you are single and are still fixated on marrying someone from your race, but there are few single men available in your culture, then you have a dilemma. You could end up waiting a long time until you finally meet someone, or you can open the playing field, socialize, and date people of other cultures.

A group acutely impacted by the scarcity of available partners is African-American women. This situation has been well documented as the result of many African-American men being incarcerated or having a criminal record. Because of the suffering some members of the African-American culture have endured at the hands of the larger society, many older African-Americans want their children to date only other African-Americans to continually reinforce the strength of the African-American legacy. This puts young, professional women in a quandary. If they follow the philosophy of their parents, they could end up alone for most, if not all, of their lives. Is cultural loyalty, though, worth a lifetime of loneliness? Should these women give up the hope of marrying and having children just to wait for the chance to marry a suitable African-American partner? Many African-American women are struggling internally with this conflict.

Stacy was one of these women. She is successful, educated, and earns a six-figure income in a conservative industry. Stacy comes from a long line of prominent dentists. She is attractive, fashionable, and has a pleasant personality. When asked whether she would date outside of her race, Stacy adamantly said no. Stacy's template was her father, who provided well for his family, was very loving, and very pro-black. The problem is that, with the shortage of available black men, Stacy has not run into anyone she considers possesses characteristics remotely similar to those of her father. On top of all that, Stacy has a job where she travels constantly and struggles to have a work/life balance. She is so tired after work she usually comes home and collapses. Her CTLAs of significant other, self-improvement, and health are severely neglected.

Since Stacy is in her mid-forties, the chance of her meeting a professional African-American man who is willing to start a family from scratch is becoming slimmer and slimmer. To increase these odds, she has to change her thinking radically. She will have to open her mind and heart to the possibility of being happy with any type of man, not just an African-American professional. Some of this subtle pressure is coming from her African-American parents, who loved and married in a different time. All they can see and preach is what it was like when they were growing up. They are not out there in today's rat race. Stacy has allowed herself to become a mule to her parents' perception of the way things should be, which is based on their own experience. Stacy has to re-adapt her values to modern society, instead of continually propagating her parents' outmoded ways of thinking. If she does not modify her social roadmap, she may very well end up alone.

So, why do women continually subjugate themselves to their parents' cultural ideals? Some may not want to deal with their parents' disapproval. Since they may already feel isolated, disapproval from their only source of support may be too much for them to take on. Another reason may be their fear of the unknown. Changing dating patterns would require women to learn a new culture. This would involve taking risks with someone who may not totally understand where they have come from. Many who work very hard on their day jobs consider this too much work to do in their private life.

Another Victorian view that some women have is waiting until they get married to buy a house. Some think that if they go ahead and buy their own house as an independent, single woman, then they are planning their lives as if they will never get married. Bridgett was one of these women. She graduated from college with a master's degree in Engineering. She liked to cook, entertain, and described herself as a "girlie girl." She was in her mid-twenties and had just started a well-paying job.

Several of her male coworkers, who also had their master's degrees in Engineering, began saving for their down payments as soon as they got their first paycheck. The company for which they worked was in a thriving high-tech college town with large predicted growth. Bridgett was afraid to talk to the bank to see if she qualified for a mortgage loan. She thought she didn't make enough money, even with her student loans, to qualify and would need two incomes, as her parents had needed when they purchased their home. She assumed her coworkers didn't have any student loans because she felt they were smarter than she was and had probably gone to college on scholarships.

After a year, two of her coworkers, Tim and Melvin, purchased modest homes with the down payments they had saved. When Bridgett talked to Tim, he mentioned that he had student loans also but qualified to get an FHA loan for his house. Bridgett felt stupid for not researching and finding out what was actually required to qualify. She began criticizing herself, saying it was now too late to buy, since housing prices had gone up because of the influx of transplants who had come to town to work at the local booming technology companies.

Chad, another engineer, started a year after Bridgett. He came in, saved for his down payment for a year, and bought a house. Bridgett sat on the sidelines and watched as Chad went through the same saving and house-purchasing process as Tim and Melvin had. Bridgett was still criticizing herself for not doing anything earlier but continued not to act. She worked at the company for five years in a town that had unprecedented growth without purchasing a home. Her male coworkers enjoyed tremendous equity growth, while Bridgett made someone else richer by paying rent. Bridgett had been a mule to her ignorance and self-doubt, instead of seeking the facts to make an informed decision.

Teresa was different than Bridgett. She worked for a year in Human Resources at a thriving company in a boomtown in the South. She brought an older, ranch-style house in a transitional—some would say questionable—neighborhood. She did minimal repairs to bring the house to a respectable condition. Two years later, she transferred to another job in Atlanta and rented out her house. She continued to get the appreciation, as well as the rent, to help cover the mortgage.

After she became engaged to her boyfriend, Chris, she sold the house at a nice profit and rolled the money into a down payment on a large $800K home in an excellent school district. After Teresa and Chris had their first child, Teresa was able to work from home part time and really enjoyed the house she and Chris had invested in. Teresa had been business savvy, while Bridgett had been paralyzed by fear and inaction. The equity that Teresa had earned as a single homeowner had been rolled over to an asset she and her new husband purchased, giving them a stronger foundation with which to begin their lives.

Another area where women can be mules to Victorian ideals is when it comes to starting a family. Most people are raised to think there is a perfect time for starting a family. Traditionalists would say that this time is after you have met Mr. Right and are married, but then the question is: what if Mr. Right hasn't shown up? Some women are in their forties and Mr. Right hasn't shown up, or else they have divorced Mr. Wrong and are alone. What should these women do?

Sheila was one of these women. She was single, successful, and a very loving person. She had been in some long-term relationships, but they just hadn't worked out. The timing for the men she had chosen was always wrong. They were either divorced, already had families and didn't want to start a second one, or they had so much "baby mamma drama" with a woman who'd had their unplanned child that they were turned off to the whole concept. Instead of cutting her losses with these men who clearly weren't keen to have more children, Sheila stayed in these relationships, hoping her suitors would be so in love with her they would change their minds.

Sheila wasted ten of her best childbearing years with guys who didn't mind wasting her time. She had been a mule to her hopeful thinking.

Fortunately, Sheila woke up in her early forties, and ended a dead-end relationship. She decided to pursue adoption and give a child a wonderful home.

Some women think very progressively. They don't let society dictate the perfect time for them to be a mother. These women who also have their own resources do not make thoughtless decisions to become a mother suddenly, like many poverty-stricken teens do today. One of these women is Angelina Jolie. She adopted her first child,

Maddox, from a Vietnamese orphanage. Then she adopted Zahara, an Ethiopian orphan. The fact that she didn't have a good man didn't stop her. She had already been married twice and both marriages hadn't worked out. She knew she couldn't center her life around what was convenient for a man or in line with the norms of society. When she met Brad Pitt, he decided to become the legal father of her kids. They have since had three of their own children. The old people used to say, "If a man loves you, he will be good to your children." This seems to be true in the Jolie/Pitt relationship.

Angelina Jolie doesn't just look like a queen in her designer clothes. She acts like a queen as well. She cares for the less fortunate and doesn't subjugate her life choices to accommodate outdated ideals.

Also, to be fair to some men, the way women may have started and raised a prior family may be important. If a woman raises a thoughtful, kind, well-mannered child, a real man will not be intimidated by the responsibility of being a stepfather to the child. If he does, then the man has more problems than just the fear of fatherhood. He may have other insecurities or a financial situation that will be centered around what he likes, instead of what his potential wife likes.

Many women may marry someone they think at the time is Mr. Right. He swears he wants to have kids and be the father his father never was, but then does an about-face once he is married. He wants to be the center of attention and, in his mind, there is no room for a child. He develops sudden amnesia about his promise to be a father to his new wife's children. What is she to do? Should she be a mule to his new point of view for the rest of her life?

Some women in some cultures are mules to their cultural identity at the expense of their own personal happiness. Some men of certain cultures selfishly ask or pressure their women to make this horrible sacrifice. One of the areas in which this behavior manifests itself is in interracial dating.

With integration, the civil rights movement, and the increase in immigration, there is a culturally diverse group of women who are maintaining their financial independence through well-paying jobs. At work and in their neighborhoods, women are socializing with people of other cultures. In some of these cases, women fall in love with people from other races. Unfortunately, a woman's family may have dreams of her marrying one of their own. This causes conflict and stress for the woman and her potential partner.

There may be many reasons for a modern working woman to desire and marry a man from another culture. The first is that the woman actually falls in love with the man as an individual, irrespective of his culture or ethnicity. They may have much in common intellectually, and the two fall in love. The movie *Something New*, starring Sanaa Latham and Simon Baker, is a Hollywood example of this trend. She was a hard-charging professional, and he owned a landscaping business. She came from a well-to-do, two-parent black family, and her father was dead set on her marrying a professional black man. When the father suspected she might be falling in love with the landscaper, he applied pressure and inflicted guilt on his daughter for wanting to abandon her culture. She became a mule to this pressure for a while, but she realized that the successful black lawyer her parents wanted her to settle down with was an insensitive jerk who was stuck on appearances and not the depth of a woman.

She gained strength and went back to Simon after she had unceremoniously dumped him. Her confidence in what she knew she wanted as a woman made her reject a choice that was culturally comfortable to her parents but emotionally empty for her.

Sanaa Latham's character was like many contemporary professional black women who are having trouble finding suitable African-American partners. Their choices are to continue sifting through few options, settle for someone less than desirable from a financial and educational standpoint, or date outside of their race. Many black professional women are choosing the latter rather than spending years being alone.

Unfortunately, the cultural dissatisfaction with a woman's dating choices can be taken to the extreme. This can result in what is called an "honor killing" when a woman falls in love or marries a man outside of the family's culture and the family feels it has been dishonored. They kill the woman in question to regain some of their honor. This can be the dreadful result of a woman exercising a choice in her life within certain cultures.

Maryam Namazie's article "Stoned to Death For Falling In Love" says that "In Britain alone, up to 17,000 women are subjected to honor-related kidnapping, sexual assault, beatings and murder every year—most of them in their very own homes and by those closest to them— their fathers, brothers, husbands, and extended family members."

Thankfully, in the United States, honor killings are a crime. But there are still families who disown their daughters or make them feel guilty for choosing to date or marry someone outside of their race. A woman has to opt for choices that will make her happy over the long run. Her family must allow her to make her choice about who to marry unencumbered. A woman should exercise her own right to do so as well.

Chapter 10:

Mule to Negative People

When a sinister person means to be your enemy, they always start by trying to be your friend.

William Blake

Today, many talk shows and books focus on positive thinking. Oprah spends time talking about it. Norman Vincent Peale wrote about it. The book *The Secret* was all about it too. So, if there is so much information out there about positive thinking, why do many women still have a problem being optimistic?

Well, negative thinking can become a habit. You think positively for a short while and then slip into self-doubt and criticism. One of the main triggers for slipping into negative thinking can be the people you surround yourself with. Being around critical people can reinforce the habit of thinking negative thoughts that many of us were raised with. Negative people eat away at your joy of life; they poison your thinking and kill your dreams. Just like a fly can spread a disease to an innocent mule, a negative person can infect a woman with a defeatist attitude, limiting her drive to succeed.

One of the key ways to correct the habit of negative thinking is to minimize the number of negative people in your life. The following self-assessment questions will show you whether you lean toward a negative frame of mind:

- Do you get more joy out of listening to a bad story than a good one?
- Does it secretly make you feel better when you hear of a friend having problems with her boyfriend or husband?
- Do you use the word "but" in your conversations with friends a lot? This is a sign that you have a habit of coming up with excuses as to why you can't do something rather than having an open mind.
- Do you always caution your friends and your family about risks or bad things that can happen to them?
- Are you drawn to grocery store tabloid magazines with gory or depressing headlines about some celebrity's embarrassment?

If you answered yes to three or more of these questions, you definitely have an affinity for negative things. This means you have to work hard to avoid the built-in tendency to gravitate toward negative people. Below are some steps to take in order to address this habit:

1. You have to go cold turkey. Remove yourself from negative people and information. You need to do this for at least a month so you can reprogram your mind to break the habit of feeding on negativity.

2. Purposely inject yourself into positive environments and conversations with positive people. At first, you may find these people less stimulating or exciting, but, over time, the interactions should feel more pleasant. A way to make these interactions more fulfilling is to develop the art of "encouragement and recommendation." This means that in every conversation you have, you encourage the person in at least one positive way. Make one useful recommendation you think may help that person's life in general or solve the problem she or he is discussing. Keep a journal on how you feel after your conversations with these people. This way, you can track your progress.

3. Family members from whom you can't get away are harder to deal with. This requires a more direct sort of action. You may not be able to eliminate them from your life since they are family. First, try to sit them down and have a talk with them about how their constant negativity turns you off and makes you want to avoid them. This may catch them by surprise. They may take in what you said with a sincere heart or react angrily to the criticism. You have to be prepared for either response. If their response is angry and abusive, you may have to limit your interactions with them to attending critical family functions, such as holiday events, funerals, birthdays, etc. They may, however, change the way they interact with you if they realize that the penalty of their negative personality is that you are around less. Pain or loneliness is a great teacher when words fail.

Why are negative people so addictive? At first, they may secretly provide comfort to our own insecurities since they are pointing out negative aspects of other, sometimes more successful, people. We all feel imperfect a lot of the time. Negative people highlight the imperfections in others. This can make us feel less isolated with our problems. The old adage "misery loves company" is not a cliché for nothing. A lot of people feel better about themselves when they see others doing just as badly.

Contemporary Americans' addiction to tabloids is a fine example of how misery loves company. In grocery stores every week, seemingly nice, happy people run to pick up the latest issue when they see a celebrity or royal family member in despair on the cover. Many shoppers read with great joy stories about the trials and tribulations of the rich and famous, with their fancy cars and fine clothes. Many of these readers enjoy thinking that even though these people are privileged, they still have down-to-earth problems. These magazines would sell very few copies if their articles didn't highlight celebrities' problems and focused instead on their successes.

The problem with negative people is that they have very little loyalty. They may talk about Sheila or Ken with you, but they may also talk about you to Sheila and Ken. You honestly have to listen to the horridness of what they say and acknowledge that they can say something just as horrible about you when you are not around. That is a fact. Talking to them is like taking a hit of a very powerful drug—it feels good when you are doing it, but it eats you up over time.

The negative friend or relative spreads pessimism, and it enters your thoughts, which reduces your energy and the amount of hope you have. It is like a disease that eats away at your happiness over the long term. Most negative people are very, very angry. They attack others verbally, putting them on the defensive. This drives would-be friends away from more cheerful companionship. Thus, the negative person spends a lot of time alone and often doesn't realize why. Such people crave true friendship and support, but they don't know how to be real friends.

Just as it is necessary to eat right and exercise to reduce our risk of cancer, it is also necessary to enact a regime to eliminate negativity from our daily lives. Some women don't minimize their interactions with critical people, and they suffer subsequent damage to their reputations. How does this occur? If you are around a person long enough, you inevitably share personal experiences or fears. Since critical people are constantly looking for more information so they can criticize, your personal disclosures provide them new fodder for criticism. They don't really care that this information is personal and sensitive to you. You are no more special than the rest of the people they talk to and make fun of.

Tina was an example of a person spewing negativity with no real loyalty to her friends. Several of Tina's entourage, who were so-called fundamentalist Christians and attended church faithfully, became fed up with Tina's negative descriptions of other people. Tina had black friends, white friends, gay friends, foreign friends, and poor friends. She was charming and could interact with people of many different social classes.

Tina's vivacious personality allowed her to make friends very easily at work, too. She would talk to her black friends about how unfair the system was at work and she would talk to her white friends about how unreliable her black friends were. She was constantly on the prowl for a man to marry, so she went to a lot of parties and social events. This allowed her to constantly add to her potential boyfriend roster and acquaintance circle. She met decent guys but was too demanding of them, which would eventually cause them to seek affection and understanding elsewhere.

Tina had the magic touch, and not just with men. She was also able to draw in women with her long list of social events and constant gossip. But the funny thing is that, just like her male friends, her female friends would get disillusioned and drop out of sight. She realized she had a problem maintaining friendships, but it never became critical because she could always replace her old friends with new ones.

Whenever her female friends seemed to be getting ahead of her (e.g., getting married or engaged), she would say something disparaging about their new mates.

Tina was able to operate this way by feeding off the emptiness in most people's lives. Many adults lives turn out to be disappointing compared to the dreams they had in college. Responsibilities, debts, and jobs all work together to make life hard and unpleasant. A woman like Tina provides fun conversation and energy, which is lacking in so many people's lives. The problem was that Tina's jovial disposition hid harsh, disloyal values. She would talk about anyone at any time to mask her own demons and to maintain an audience.

Women like Tina play chess with other people's lives. They tell one person about a particularly bad thing or they tell another about something else to incite fear and elicit a certain reaction. They may even stir the pot by telling this friend what another friend said about them. People like Tina are dark and caustic. If you suspect any of your current friends or family members are like this, stay away from them as much as you can. You will deal with enough negative people at work, so why invite them into your home life?

As mentioned earlier, when the toxic comments come from a family member, this makes it all the harder to quarantine them from your life. Leslie grew up in a middle-class home with an educated mother and a blue-collar father. The mother secretly resented the husband she had chosen and took it out on the whole family. As Leslie grew up, she never really heard her mother say anything that was really kind or nice. Leslie was always too skinny, too lazy, too tomboyish, or she asked too many questions.

Leslie wasn't the only one targeted by her mother, though. Because her mother hated her job, she talked badly about her coworkers, but she wouldn't leave her work. She called any independent woman she ran into a whore. She would constantly sit in front of the television looking for bad characters to obsess over.

She constantly told Leslie most men were unreliable and that Leslie would always have to depend on herself. She didn't limit her criticism to others, though. She constantly talked about being fired or being too fat, too shy, or too poor. In essence, she was a very unhappy woman.

As a young child, Leslie couldn't do much about her situation, but as an adult, she started building her own support system of pleasant friends. She felt happier and more adventurous. She took trips and met even more new people. Leslie basically built a new life. Her mother would complain that Leslie had forgotten where she had come from. Leslie hadn't forgotten, but she was trying her best to. Leslie was smart. She focused on her future rather than allowing an anchor from the past to be tied to her leg.

Unfortunately, many young women are exposed to negative influences outside the home. Many of today's high schools are a breeding ground for destructive peer pressure and low self-esteem. Melissa was a shy, bright sophomore. She had a critical mother and a father who worked two jobs. She knew getting high grades was her ticket out of her parents' house and into a good college. She studied hard and actually enjoyed reading, especially history and literature books.

At school, her more popular peers, such as the jocks, cheerleaders, and really attractive girls with whom the guys were trying to have sex, were protected from ugly comments. The less popular students had to face the terror of being ridiculed as they got on and off the school bus. Sometimes, the guys on the bus would even reach out and squeeze a body part. Melissa spoke to her parents about how she hated riding the school bus, but they told her they had to work and couldn't leave and drive all the way over to pick her up. Melissa looked forward to turning sixteen so she could persuade her dad to buy her an old beat-up car she could drive herself.

Riding the school bus wasn't Melissa's only anxious situation. She also hung out in a clique at school. The girl who led the clique, Jackie, was part of the "in crowd" because she had a good figure and many of the guys wanted to date her. At first, Melissa felt that as long as she was in Jackie's clique, she would be okay until she graduated. But Melissa began to realize that Jackie controlled the girls in her clique by mentally intimidating them. Jackie's best friend, Lori, was in the clique too. Lori was tall, ugly, and had a body that looked like a man's, which is probably why insecure Jackie had her as a best friend. Plus,

Lori had a brother who was a popular senior, which gave the group some clout by association.

Melissa felt Jackie and Lori were constantly scrutinizing her. They talked about her hair, clothes, and the way she walked. Jackie would make fun of her, sometimes in front of the other girls, and it made Melissa feel bad. She began dreading going to school, although she knew it was her way out of her unhappy home and into an independent future. She even had to ride the bus with Lori and another girl in the clique named Sheila. Sheila was part of a second-marriage package—her father had retained custody of her when Sheila's mother moved to New York to start over. The stepmother didn't really want her new, ready-made family; she just wanted Sheila's father, so she pretended to like Sheila until they got married. Sheila's stepmother acted reasonably when the father was at home, but when he went to work, she bossed Sheila around and verbally abused her. Sheila had a lot of built-up resentment about her stepmother and felt abandoned by her real mother. Sheila brought her anger and aggression right to high school and took it out on the weaker girls in the clique, including Melissa. She picked on Melissa at every opportunity, making fun of her hair, her smile, and the way she walked. Melissa felt awkward enough, but Sheila made it unbearable. Melissa became the mule of Sheila and Lori's jokes on the school bus. They would pick on Melissa to make the boys on the bus laugh so they wouldn't pick on them. Melissa went through this hell for an entire year until summer.

When July arrived, Melissa turned sixteen and her father followed through on his promise and bought her a car. She convinced Pam and Dee, two of the weaker girls in the clique (who also got picked on) to ride with her and abandon the clique. They felt relieved to have an option outside of the constant terrorizing they had endured at the hands of Jackie and her clique. They all rode to school together and found their own little spot to congregate. Jackie's ego was bruised. She tried to harass them, but there really was nothing she could do. Melissa had taken her own destiny into her hands at sixteen, eliminating the poison that Jackie had brought into her and the two other girls' lives.

Women like Jackie and Melissa aren't limited to high schools—they are in churches, country clubs, and charity organizations across the country. Many women who are hurt by other things in their lives take their anger out on innocent bystanders all the time. Many young women are victims of emotionally abusive environments and don't even realize it. They just think it's tough love or that maybe there's something wrong with them that warrants the unfair treatment. Damaged, vulnerable women can be cruel, nasty creatures. Some thrive on putting others down to make themselves feel better. No matter how good you look or how kind you are to them, it will never be enough to make them treat you with respect. They have personal demons they haven't addressed yet. They get a quick high from insulting people behind their backs and sometimes in front of others to create a temporary sense of power and self-worth. Don't hang out in the dungeon with these women. Elevate yourself and move on as fast as you can. Being a mule to these types of women means wasting your life.

Unlike Jackie, there are women who have such bright spirits that they elevate others by listening to them and offering heartfelt advice. Henrietta is a good example of such a "spiritual queen." She was open-minded, welcoming, and nonjudgmental. This tolerance attracted people of all faiths, from fundamentalist Christians to atheists, for counseling. Friends who sought her guidance ranged from high-flying executives to recovering addicts.

After college, she held many jobs, such as weight-loss counselor, suicide hotline operator, and substitute teacher. She had grown up in a home with very punitive religious beliefs and had felt stifled as a child. As an adult, she became a member of a very open, tolerant religious discipline. It allowed her to see the world in a much broader way. She is always calm and centered in a place of love. People are drawn to her because they know they will receive emotional comfort.

The people with whom you spend a lot of time are a reflection of how you feel about yourself. If you want to feel good about yourself, surround yourself with happy people. Some people's lives are so empty that their main hobby is talking about people. You never hear these people saying they are working on a project or a hobby. These folks also do very little charity work because they are self-absorbed and insecure.

To test the quality of your friendships, try the following:

1. List three things that happened in your life that you are ashamed of.
2. Next, make a list of your ten closest family members or friends.
3. From your list, write down the names of the people who, if they knew the three things you are most ashamed of, would still treat you the same and never use it to embarrass you.

4. If you have no friends who wouldn't judge you or use the information in a negative way, you need to clean out your friendship closet and replace them with people you choose who have a better spirit.
5. If you have no family members on that list, including your spouse, then you need to seriously consider building a surrogate family that will be supportive.

What kind of friends does a queen have?

• She has friends with a sense of humor.
• She has both male and female friends.
• She has friends that celebrate her achievements.
• She doesn't have friends who constantly talk about people.
• She has friends in towns other than where she lives.
• She has friends who have interests other than shopping.

You deserve good friends. They are worth more than any amount of money you could ever earn. They visit when you are sick, listen to you when you are sad, and celebrate with you when you are happy. Don't settle for less. Dodge and dump the ones you can't afford to be unguarded around.

Chapter 11:

Mule to Whining

The dog barks, but the caravan moves on.

Arabic Proverb

It's sad to say, but even in the twenty-first century, there are women who whine to get what they want. Like a mule, they don't break free and establish their own path. They whine when things aren't going their way, waiting for someone else to liberate them. Whining women are needy and manipulative—they are not people who are competent and intelligent. If such a woman has the shortsighted goal of just getting what she wants, then, in time, she will lose respect. So, why do so many educated women resort to this behavior?

Many fathers think their daughters are "special" or "perfect." Most children, however, are geniuses at using certain behavior to get what they want from their parents. Consequently, a common pattern some girls develop is whining to their fathers about a problem and causing him to come to the rescue. Many fathers like to be their daughter's "knight in shining armor"; however, this behavior by many fathers teaches their young daughters that they can be rewarded for whining. Some women take this lesson right on into adulthood.

Whining damages your relationships, and, in most work environments, it is the kiss of death. When people have a dialogue with an adult woman, they are not expecting to deal with a hopelessly childlike person. When a woman whines, she puts the responsibility for her happiness and problem solving onto someone else instead of taking on that responsibility herself. Basically, this is a cop-out. More specifically, though, let's examine the payoffs and problems of using whining to manipulate others and cause a certain outcome.

Kerry was a chirpy, attractive blonde who had graduated from a respected liberal arts college. Her first job was at a small consulting firm with an overabundance of men. She was a neat dresser and spoke well to sound impressive. However, there was a problem when Kerry went to a client site. She preferred to dictate orders rather than get her hands dirty with the details. She didn't like crunching numbers for hours and poring over spreadsheets. Straining her eyes and brain to put effective presentations together depressed her.

So, how did Kerry skirt work on a client's assignment? When she arrived, she would learn who signed off the budget. That person would become the target of her manipulation. Whenever she wanted to avoid work, she would complain to the sponsor that she wasn't getting the support she needed from the company's lower minions. The sponsor would empathize, pushing his team to work harder to provide Kerry the documentation she needed. Kerry made sure she always complimented the commitment of the sponsor in her status updates to his management. Flattery got her everywhere. Thus, Kerry never had to do any "real" work.

This game worked for Kerry for a while, until one of the female minions Kerry had backstabbed replaced the sponsor to whom she had whined. As a result, Kerry ended up getting a bad recommendation from her new sponsor. Ultimately, her contract wasn't renewed, which led her to look elsewhere for her next assignment.

Why did Kerry rely on manipulation to get ahead? Maybe, since that pattern was reinforced repeatedly when she was a child, she didn't think she could succeed any other way. Even though a woman may have impressive degrees, her self-confidence may not be what it needs to be in order to apply herself fully in the corporate world.

Kerry's father had rewarded her for whining. As a little girl, when she encountered a problem, she would run to her father and he would solve it for her. He even sold her Girl Scout cookies for her. He let himself become a mule to Kerry's whining. This subconsciously programmed her to expect other men to make themselves mules to her whining. If she ever happened to come across a male in a corporate environment who had daughters who whined, Kerry would have some degree of success. However, if she came across a hard-charging manager or a woman, these tactics would fail very quickly. Kerry needs to be in the latter environment so she can develop the skills to legitimately achieve results. This will serve her career better in the long run.

Weak women also tend to use whining in spousal relationships. Cindy was a wife who used whining to her advantage, or so she thought. She was a southern belle who had been raised to think a woman had to let the man think he was smarter—not some of the time, but all of the time. When her husband, Dirk, would come home on Fridays from being on the road with a high-powered consulting firm, Cindy would immediately start whining about stupid things the kids had done or household chores she wanted him to do. This seemed cute to him for a while. However, Cindy's husband began feeling a lot of pressure to bring new business to his firm after being made a partner. At that point, Cindy's whining began to grate on his nerves. He would spend longer and longer amounts of time away from home. Instead of coming home on Fridays, he started coming home every other week. This made Cindy more anxious, causing her to whine and question Dirk even more when she finally did see him.

Dirk couldn't afford to leave Cindy. They had three children. He didn't want his check decimated by child support and alimony payments to a wife who had never worked. He didn't really communicate to Cindy what the problem was. Avoidance was Dirk's coping mechanism. As the kids got older, they even began to resent the times when he did come home and enforce household rules on them. He eventually quit even trying. This caused his son to drift listlessly from one college to another trying to find himself. The two girls, however, had more discipline and did well in school. Nonetheless, they repeated Cindy's patterns of whining with their professors and managers wherever they worked.

Whining to men can seem to many women like an effective way of getting what they want, but women also whine to their female friends. This has one of two effects on the relationship. If a female friend has a nurturing tendency, then she becomes the mule to the whiner. This type of friendship becomes very unpleasant to the "listener." If the female friend has little tolerance for whining, then the friendship becomes strained or simply ends.

Greg Behrendt and Liz Tuccillo's book *He's Just Not That Into You* highlights how women love to make excuses for men with bad behavior. Some women's habit of making excuses, though, plays right into a whiner's hands. The whiner senses that she or he will never be held accountable, and the friend gets drained while providing solutions and suggestions that the whiner is not really interested in hearing. The "kryptonite" to a whiner is accountability or action.

Angela had a large group of girlfriends she talked to often. However, Angela started to dread hearing her phone ring. She felt guilty because one of her friends, Kate, always seemed to have problems. She had one problem after another at her job. Kate would call Angela on the weekend and go on and on about them. The weekend was Angela's downtime, and these conversations would remind Angela of her own problems on the job.

Kate's world was pretty small because she didn't have kids. Basically, all she had was her job and her husband, but the problem was that Kate couldn't talk to her husband about her job problems. He wasn't professional and, therefore, couldn't relate. He felt that Kate should just confront people head-on, like he did in his blue-collar business. He would get frustrated when Kate would go on and on without solving her problems with her coworkers. So, when her husband began turning a deaf ear, Kate turned to Angela.

At first, Angela empathized with Kate about her job issues since she also had these issues. But, eventually, she found that Kate would have one problem after another with her female coworkers. When Angela tried to help her solve those problems, Kate would rarely apply any of the strategies Angela recommended. Instead, she would come back with the very same problems week after week.

Another frustrating thing about listening to Kate was that Angela could never get any feedback on her problems. She was always in listening mode. When she brought up a work issue she had, Kate would listen superficially for a minute, then turn the conversation right back to something about her. Angela listened for months, but then she decided not to pick up her phone on weekends.

Why had Angela let Kate use her in this way? Well, first she felt guilty about not being there for her friend when she was needed. Angela had job problems herself, so she knew how difficult dealing with office politics could be. The problem was that Kate never worked really hard to solve her problems or change jobs. She just complained continually about work. Her husband was not much help financially because Kate was the primary breadwinner. Angela felt this added to Kate's stress and that she should be there for Kate.

What Angela began to realize was that she was being a mule to Kate's whining even though Kate wouldn't listen to her for very long. When she realized how unfair Kate was being, it made her feel angry and cheated. Ultimately, when Angela decided to stop feeding Kate's whining and stopped answering her phone on the weekend, Kate started complaining that Angela was difficult to catch up with. What Angela heard Kate saying was basically, "How dare you have a life outside of my needs?" Angela decided to prioritize the enjoyment of her free time rather than place Kate's needs over hers.

This decision freed Angela from her resentment and caused Kate to address some of her work issues directly instead of relying on Angela as a crutch. People who use you only do so if you let them. Cut off the friend who whines by offering solutions that are direct and to the point. If they don't listen, cut the conversation short and find something better to do with your time. Never, ever, let a whiner repeatedly steal your quality time. Most people have CTLAs they need to attend to.

One of the most common forms of whining is when a child whines to a parent. We are all familiar with that. But sometimes the roles can reverse as a parent ages. A parent may be alone after their kids have gone off to college. They may have stayed married to someone with whom they have very little in common. A parent's life can feel empty. Some may count on their children to fill that emptiness. The tool they often use to coerce a child into investing more time at home is guilt-inducing whining.

This tactic causes anxiety in grown children who are trying to establish their own adult lives for the first time. They constantly have to worry about Mommy or Daddy when they are trying to get their first apartment, first house, first job, first husband, and so one. Is this fair? No, it isn't, but that doesn't stop any self-absorbed parent from whining to get the attention they want.

If an adult child avoids the parent because of this unpleasant whining, the parent may increase their amount of phone calls until the adult child caves in. This adds additional stress to the already chaotic lives of many young adults. With high-pressure jobs, crazy traffic, and mounting bills after college, a parent's guilt-tripping is a heavy burden for many young adults to carry.

Parents may go as far as whining to other relatives about how their children don't visit them. The other relatives may sometimes intervene and call the wayward child with new guilt-trips. This causes even more resentment in the adult child. They start to feel bullied. It's as if their thoughts and feelings don't count. They are being made a mule to their parent's lack of strength or poor choices, which prevents them from having a more fulfilling life.

There is even a term for parents who start this intrusive behavior while the child is in college. They are called "helicopter parents." On August 3, 2008, Wikepedia had the following definition:

> A "helicopter parent" is a term for a person who pays extremely close attention to his or her child or children, particularly at educational institutions. They rush to prevent any harm or failure from befalling them or letting them learn from their own mistakes, sometimes even contrary to the children's wishes. They are so named because, like a helicopter, they hover closely overhead, rarely out of reach whether their children need them or not.

The cell phone allows people to be readily accessible anytime and any place. If one of your parents is a bored helicopter parent, your life may be bombarded by unwanted phone calls and batteries of questions. This can be extremely irritating to a grown child who is exploring the exciting world at college or trying to establish his or her independence for the first time.

Email is another mechanism some parents use to invade their child's life, without even talking to them. Some adult children receive emails with long lists of questions or complaints. Frequent emails from parents can cause anxiety.

With the advance of technology, it is becoming harder for children to take adequate breaks from parents seeking to impose on their time. People are carrying handheld devices through which emails can be received at any time of the day. The only way to deal with a parent addicted to sending emails is to skip over these emails.

Helicopter parents intrude into their kid's lives to help them solve problems. However, what this does is actually prevent young adults from strengthening their ability to face their own challenges. To sharpen a coping skill, it has to be used when mistakes are made. If parents are always coming to their kids' rescue, the proper skills never develop.

This is also extremely selfish parental behavior because if a parent dies, the adult child needs to be equipped enough to build his or her own life. They also will need problem-solving skills when they marry another person. Every marriage has challenges, and both parties have to work through sticky issues together. If one person is inept at doing this, he or she may rely on the other person in the relationship to make most decisions, even if this sometimes seems not to be in their best interest.

No parent should want to cripple their child's growth, and that is exactly what interfering and whining does—it doesn't allow children to develop their own lives or think for themselves.

Why would parents purposely invade their children's lives without a thought about their right to privacy? Loneliness. Selfishness. Boredom. Some parents participate in no projects of their own that would provide meaning in their lives. However, what these parents are missing is the realization that, in order to inspire people to want to spend time with them, the interactions have to be pleasant. They can't be filled with endless questioning and complaining. Thoughtful behavior towards others attracts people; selfish behavior repels.

How does a queen feel about whining?

- She doesn't have many friends who whine.
- She has no time for whiners because she is too busy living life.
- She doesn't use it as a tool against men.

Overall, whining is a manipulative tactic that some use to receive attention. Many fall into a whiner's trap and spend endless hours listening to a person who will never take real action to solve her or his problems. Being a mule to someone else's whining means that you are wasting your time and not solving your own problems. Naturally, everyone has down periods, and you can provide an empathetic ear for a few conversations, but if you see a pattern, tell that person that you feel burdened. If they get angry or don't change their behavior, cut your losses and move on.

Chapter 12:

Mule to Your Hair

I like talking. I didn't know at the time I would have to worry so much about my hair.

Diane Sawyer

No one can deny that beautiful hair is attractive. Christie Brinkley, Farrah Fawcett, and Jennifer Aniston all have famous manes. Even short hair can make an unforgettable statement. Short haircuts helped catapult Halle Berry, Dorothy Hamill, and Sinead O'Connor to celebrity status. Clearly, beautiful hair in women attracts men.

However, it must be remembered that in addition to the extensive media coverage these female celebrities enjoy, they have access to the best stylists daily. Many ordinary working women try to emulate celebrities in their choice of hairstyles, but in today's society some women are mules to their hair. They wash, spray, tease, blow-dry, flat-iron, color, cut, straighten, and perm their hair in an effort to look glamorous.

Some women with long daily commutes get up an hour earlier just to do their hair. They wash, blow-dry, curl, and style it all before heading off to work. Imagine doing this an hour a day for the rest of your adult life. That is time you could spend exercising or eating a healthy, unrushed breakfast.

Susan would exercise in the morning; come back to her apartment; shower; wash, blow-dry, and style her hair; and then head off to catch the train for an hour commute. By the time she got to work, she was exhausted. It took her thirty minutes to calm down enough to focus on work.

Susan knew there had to be a better way. Daily hair preparation was stressing her out. In winter, when she caught the train, her hair was wet because she hadn't had time to dry it. She asked her friend Tina for advice. Tina told her to switch her exercise routine to the evenings after work. The new routine wasn't perfect, but it removed some stress from Susan's mornings.

Why do women invest so much time maintaining their hair? One reason is that many of them regard their hair as key to their attractiveness. Some consider hair even more important than personality, intelligence, makeup, or clothes. They want it shiny, bouncy, and devoid of gray. Some even believe the Bible indicates a woman's hair is important. Corinthians 11:15 says, "But if a woman has long hair, it is a glory to her: for her hair is given her for covering."

So, how can a woman sport attractive hair without spending an hour a day on it? First, she should invest in a top-notch haircut. If she receives a great style that is low maintenance, she can look stylish and save a lot of time in daily preparation. Second, if she is wedded to long hair, she can pull her hair back in a chic ponytail and be on her way. On weekends, when she is more likely to go out socializing, she can indulge herself by investing time in a comprehensive curling, blow-drying, and styling routine.

One way to save time is not to wash your hair every day, unless you are exercising or swimming. You can wash it every other day and retain more of the natural oils to make the hair naturally shiny.

Emulating a celebrity hairstyle can also be useful if it is low maintenance. Many women in the '70s requested Dorothy Hamill's haircut by Vidal Sassoon. It looked great and required very little maintenance. Examine a variety of celebrities and see which ones have both an attractive and low-maintenance hairstyle. Review magazines such as *Style*, *Vogue*, *Harper's Bazaar*, and *Essence* for trendy, easy-to-maintain styles. Take a picture of your desired haircut to a talented local hairstylist and ask her or him to replicate the look.

One hairstyle that has withstood the test of time is the bob—it always looks classy and pulled together and is preferred by many rich, high-society women. It is low on maintenance, always looks professional, and you can wear it short or long. Dorothy Hamill's haircut was a feathered variation of the bob.

Some women have a mule-like stubbornness they flaunt by wearing the same out-dated hairstyle for years. They tend to cling to a hairstyle they adopted during a fun time of their lives and hold on to it even if it is outdated or requires a lot of care. Keeping an updated, low-maintenance look is essential for the modern woman. If you haven't changed your hair in four years or more, you may be trapped in the past. Good examples of this are all those women who are on the makeover shows. Everyone seems to know they need a new hairstyle except them. Once they receive the fresh haircut, it is amazing how much better most of these women look. They are usually highly resistant to change all the way up to the time they sit in the stylist's chair. They are probably resistant to other changes in their lives as well.

Conversely, while many African-American women change their hairstyles often, they still remain mules to the styling of their hair. Since their hair has natural curl, many spend a lot of time, chemicals, and money getting it straight. Many became liberated from the straightening routines in the '70s and grew Afros. This lasted a while until there was a large influx of blacks into corporate America. Then, many black women decided to straighten their hair in order to fit in better with their Caucasian peers.

Today, most African-American women schedule weekly or bi-weekly appointments with their hairdressers. In between these times, many get up early just to do their hair. They curl, moisturize, and style their hair every day. Many feel under great pressure to have an attractive head of hair. In the African-American culture, there can be an "unspoken" penalty for having an unkempt head. African-American men may consider such women ungroomed. Women may say you look shabby because hair is such a focal point of this cultural group in particular.

In the '80s, a number of professionals, including some busy African-American actresses who had stylists, invested in weaves. "Weave" is a term for adding artificial or real hair from someone else to your own. The hair is usually a straight grade that makes everyday maintenance easy to manage. The practice became so popular many Caucasian actresses, models, and entertainers started getting weaves and extensions too. Britney Spears, Jessica Simpson, and a lot of runway models regularly sport extensions due to the constant styling, washing, and drying from bright lights that their hair has to endure.

Some progressive black women have decided to opt out of the whole styling game by going to short, natural haircuts or braids. Ten years ago, braids would have been totally unacceptable in a corporate environment. Today, however, corporate tolerance for personal hair preferences has progressed to the stage where many African-American women feel comfortable coming to work with a short haircut or braids. The styles require almost no daily maintenance and need only be refreshed or tightened every six weeks on average.

How does a queen have great hair without hassle?

- She has a stylish cut.
- She has a stylist who asks her about her lifestyle *before* she cuts her hair.
- She doesn't keep the same hairstyle for more than four years.

Whatever your hair situation, find a convenient way to style your hair that does not make inroads on your time. You rule your hair; don't let your hair rule you.

Chapter 13:

Mule to Routine

The less routine, the more life.

Amos Bronson Alcott

For many people, doing the same things over and over again gives them the comfort of predictability. Routine is part of everyone's lives. Our routines include going to work, attending church, checking in with old friends, paying bills, and so on. But sometimes routine can be dangerous. You can grow stale or narrow-minded by not exploring new interests. Some people become stuck in unfulfilling relationships because they are more married to their routines than they are to each other. You can become intellectually lazy after earning a degree if no further training is acquired. Your brain grows stale if you don't keep feeding and testing it.

Unfortunately, many women allow themselves to become mules to their routines. Like a mule trudging up the same hill every day, some women don't introduce much variation into their lives. They perform the same household chores and extracurricular activities, interacting with the same people day after day. Some are even closed off and judgmental when talking with new people that seem different. These women relax into a tenuous sort of comfort zone, thinking they know what will happen. This sense of comfort is turned on its head if they get a terminal disease, lose their job, or go through a divorce. Inevitably, circumstance forces them to build a new set of routines.

Why do so many women (and men) cling to routine? A lot of this clinging is driven by fear. Some women have been socialized with a fear of taking chances. We may fear dating many people because this could be viewed as promiscuous. So often, we settle for one person who may not be compatible, but whom we know well. We may be scared to travel alone because of things we have been told about our personal safety. Consequently, we travel only when others are ready to accompany us. Or perhaps we build our lives around raising children, and then, when they go off to college, our lives are bleak and empty.

To most women, routines feel safe, but always playing it safe can stunt your growth. Some women feel that playing it safe protects them from rejection. However, if you talk to some successful businessmen or millionaires, you will find that many had business failures before they hit the big time. Simon Cowell, of *American Idol* fame, failed at his first attempt to establish the music company E&S. Oprah Winfrey was rejected when she applied for her first television anchor spot. Similarly, many famous writers have been rejected by major publishing houses before becoming successful. Mary Higgins Clark had her novel, *Journey Back To Love,* rejected. Stephen King's novel, *Carrie,* was rejected by a publisher before it went on to become a bestseller. He became the bestselling American author of all time.

These famous people all had to operate outside of a routine or safety zone to ultimately achieve their dreams. They each went on to be wildly successful. Often we just see the successful end products and we think the people who created them were always revered for their talent, but if you talked to each one of them you would see that many were made to feel bad about their looks or were criticized for their craft. They could have caved in and listened to how they should have been content with the way things were. They didn't, though, and they went on to accomplish extraordinary achievements.

Doing the same routine over and over again feels safe, but there are no guarantees. Many American workers employed in the same job for twenty years or more still get laid off. Some women support their husbands in the early days of their careers and are then dumped for somebody else. Some women who exercise regularly still die of a heart attack or stroke. Others have put tender loving care into fixing up their houses only to see them destroyed by floods, hurricanes, or other natural disasters. So, as you can see, operating in a routine does not always guarantee stability.

Celeste is a woman who played it safe. After graduating from college, she met and married a nice man, Frank. He was a blue-collar worker who went to work every day to provide for his family. Even though his job was physically challenging, the day-to-day stress of racism on the job wore him down. He would talk to Celeste about his problems, but he didn't really want to burden her since she had her hands full caring for their kids, so Frank kept most of his stress to himself.

Celeste also worked outside of the home as a teacher. She didn't earn much money, but Frank had a good income, so she never really worried. Celeste thought they enjoyed a good life. Frank made enough money to pay the bills because they lived very modestly. Frank would work overtime to provide money for any needs the kids had growing up. Celeste appreciated having a good man to take care of the family. Many of her friends had husbands who drank or cheated on them. Most of these friends were depressed and overweight from the unhappiness their husbands had brought into their homes. Celeste, on the other hand, had gained only a few pounds since high school and, overall, kept a pleasant demeanor.

The one thing Celeste did overlook was that Frank had long periods of withdrawal. He would come home from work and shut down. He attributed this to the stress of the day. Celeste decided to leave Frank alone rather than probe deeper and try to help him.

Their kids eventually left the house and went off to college. Frank and Celeste had saved money, which enabled them to pay for their children's undergraduate education. The kids would come home for visits about once a month, but they were basically out of the house for good.

Unlike many couples, Celeste and Frank enjoyed their empty nest. They were able to spend more quiet time alone with less day-to-day pressures. All Frank could talk about was how much he was looking forward to retiring. He wanted to spend more time at home. The politics and racism he encountered on the job were really wearing him down.

However, within one year of retiring, Frank dropped dead of a heart attack. His life insurance and pension were able to pay off most of the bills, which prevented any major financial worries for Celeste, but Celeste became very lonely. She was in her upper fifties and had many older female friends through her social club. Unfortunately, good friends could not fill the void of a caring husband.

Celeste felt some guilt about Frank. She knew his heart attack may have been triggered by his job stress. Before his death she had always believed he was strong enough to handle this stress. She realized she had probably been a little too comfortable in her lifestyle, for she had never urged her husband to seek help for his bouts of depression. She also realized she may not have done her part in looking out for his overall health.

Her social club filled some of her extra time with travel and parties, but it did not replace her husband. At her age, it was hard to find a single, eligible man in his fifties or sixties. She dated a few men, but they turned out to be duds. They were self-absorbed and tacky. All they cared about was having sex with no commitment. They never invested enough time to get to know her properly. She faced the fact that Frank's death had left her with the prospect of spending a large portion of her life alone.

Then, a couple of years later, Celeste was struck with breast cancer, which necessitated terrible bouts of chemotherapy. Her daughter tried to come home as often as she could, but she was in school studying and taking exams. There was only so much time available for her to visit her mom.

After many rough months of treatment and a mastectomy, Celeste was able to recover from her bout with breast cancer. The experience of Frank's death, along with her own illness, made Celeste feel very alone in the world. She wondered how she had ended up in such a place with possibly twenty to thirty years of life in front of her. She had never imagined a life without her husband.

Celeste had become a mule to her comfortable life-style. She had taken having a dutiful husband for granted. He had exhibited signs of needing help, but Celeste had continually overlooked them and kept on going with their well-ordered life. She should have prodded him more to seek professional help. Even if that meant he would have had to change jobs for a less stressful work environment with a resultant decline in their standard of living, at least it may have extended his lifespan.

Married women aren't the only ones who become mules to routine. In the dating arena, many single pro-fessional women complain about not being able to meet eligible men, but they never go anywhere to meet them. They go to work, where most of the men are married and supporting families. Single men in the workplace are of-ten scarce, and many of them may be confirmed bachelors or divorced men playing the field. Many women go out in packs because they feel safe. They don't feel comfort-able socializing alone, so they don't engage in one-on-one conversations with new people.

Another self-defeating practice women seeking part-ners engage in is to hang up under their families. Spending time with family is great and necessary for a healthy life, but if you are with them constantly and don't go out on your own socially, you are limiting your chances of meet-ing someone. You may have the occasional introduction by a family member, but that is rare. You are pretty much on your own in terms of finding a mate. These women ne-glect the CTLA of personal relationships/significant other and invest too much time in the CTLA of family.

Victoria and her mother were close. After she broke up with her live-in love of three years, Victoria began spending more time with her mother. She and her mother would spend most Saturdays at various malls in town looking at the latest styles.

They even planned vacations together and went on trips to Europe to shop in beautiful boutiques. When some of Victoria's friends tried to schedule weekend outings or events to meet guys, Victoria would say she couldn't participate because she already had plans with her mother.

After her mother had married and given birth to Victoria and her brother, Victoria's father died. Her mother hadn't had any dating prospects in years. Victoria knew her mother was lonely and therefore included her in all her plans.

When Victoria hit her late thirties, however, she began to panic. She realized she hadn't built up a real social life after breaking up with her boyfriend, Jake. Now, she was hanging out with her mother on weekends. She knew now that if she was ever going to marry, she would have to change the way she spent her spare time. Her comfortable routine on weekends had done nothing to get her any dates over the past year.

Women love companionship and being listened to. That is the trap Victoria had let herself fall into. Spending time around her mother was okay, but she spent too much time with her, at the expense of her own social life. She had become a mule to her mother's loneliness and avoided facing her own.

Suddenly, though, Victoria decided to make a change. She registered for a singles cruise. She decided to take a night course at the local community college, where she could meet some new people. She also started participating in some of the social outings her friends planned.

She began letting people know she was single. She even went out on some blind dates. They hadn't delivered Mr. Right yet, but she had some fun dating and was happy that at least she was out there, trying.

For Victoria, liberating herself didn't mean abandoning her mother. It just meant not letting her mother monopolize all of her free time. It allowed her to develop an independent life.

How does a queen keep from being a slave to routine?

- She engages in social activities with people her age.
- She doesn't have the same social life as her parents.
- She takes classes to learn new things.
- She tries new foods and visits new places.
- She doesn't think Mr. Right is going to come to her front door.

Many women fall into the routine of being around certain people because it provides comfort and support. What they have to learn is that you have to adapt to new situations. This allows you to be less dependent on a few companions and more open to many.

Chapter 14 :

Mule to Gossip

Avoid inquisitive persons, for they are sure to to be gossips, their ears are open to hear, but they will not keep what is entrusted to them.

HORACE

One of the most empty, nonproductive ways a woman can spend her time is by gossiping. It is a way of privately humiliating another person. The gossiper also gets a high by reporting some tidbit nobody else knows about. Spewing salacious talk gives such people a sense of power. If it is widely known that gossiping can be destructive, the question is then, why do so many women love to gossip?

Women generally have a stronger need to communicate with others than men. Part of what makes them feel validated is to have someone listen to them. There are many ways to get people to listen to you. You can motivate them by appealing to their high ideals. You can offer help to them on a specific problem they may be facing. You can tell jokes and make them laugh. But you can also appeal to their feelings of inadequacy by putting down others who may have run into misfortune. Gossip is one way a woman can get an insecure woman's attention.

What a gossiper wants is the focus of others. She uses gossip as the vehicle to become the daily focal point of her friends. It provides excitement to the gossiper and those who listen to her. If you peel apart the life of a woman who gossips, it is usually empty, boring, and miserable. A woman often gossips to compensate for the lack of variety in her own life.

It is nearly impossible to be a "true" friend of a gossiper. Gossiping is like an addiction. Gossips eventually talk about their friends as well as their foes. Subconscious anxiety arises in those dealing with a gossiper. At some level, people never really trust a gossiper. Therefore, a gossiper's friends tend to be superficial. They invest the wrong kind of activity in their CTLA of personal relationships.

Some women hang around a woman they don't even like just to get the latest gossip. Like a mule subject to the whims of its owner, a woman who associates with a gossip is subjugating herself to someone whose loyalty is razor thin. Along with the gossip, they laugh and rejoice at the catastrophes of others. These women also tend to be hypocritical, often being guilty of the same things about which they are judgmental.

For instance, Cindy was a poisonous gossip. She talked constantly about people on her cell phone. In fact, her continual cell phone gossip while driving led to several near accidents. She would be very helpful to a potential friend until the friend felt comfortable opening up to her. Then she would proceed to make that friend feel special by telling titillating rumors about people they both knew.

The juicy gossip was enough to draw in new alliances, but what these people didn't know was that Cindy, pretending she cared about a particular friend, would extract personal bits of information. Once she had secured private details about her friends' lives, she would share the information with her whole social circle.

When Cindy's friends began to realize how destructive her behavior was, they disassociated from her one by one. On some level, she acknowledged she had a gossiping problem, but she still kept on doing it.

Cindy's gossiping habit stemmed from her need for attention. She had been an only child and the apple of her parents' eyes, and this need continued well into adulthood. Her continual need for attention was satisfied by the delivery of juicy stories. She was always replacing old friends with new ones because she would constantly reel in people interested in getting the inside scoop.

Cindy's circle had two types of mules. Cindy was a mule to the need for attention. Unfortunately, she developed a destructive way of being rewarded with that attention. Cindy's revolving circle of friends became mules to her gossip. They couldn't pass up the dish Cindy was offering until it burned them. As long as it didn't touch them, they were all bought in.

After naïvely sharing information with a gossip, how does a woman safely extricate herself from that person? She has to stop sharing any new personal information immediately. This change in behavior will catch the gossip's attention. The gossip hasn't changed, so she may try to coax new information from her friend. As long as the friend doesn't comply, she may respect her friend's new boundaries. Because the friend is no longer feeding the gossiping mill, the gossip may distance herself from the friend. She may consider the friend less fun or less worthy of spending time with. This should be just fine with a woman intent on turning over a new leaf.

Some women may say things such as "I have some personal matters I am dealing with." Some may say "I'm trying to gossip less" or use the religious excuse "I'm saved." These kinds of remarks may make the gossip temporarily uncomfortable, but she may respect the friend's new behavior in the long run.

Refusing to fuel the gossip mill can cause some temporary isolation, but the vacancy will be filled with people who are more serious and focused. If they operate from a core of integrity, they will be more of a pleasure to be around in the long run.

A positive thing that may come from removing yourself from the gossip circle is that you may actually become more productive. The spare time you may have spent on the phone listening to gossip can be used for self-improvement—an important CTLA for a complete life.

Lynn used to be on the phone with Rita for hours, talking about coworkers. This went on for a couple of years. Lynn began to notice that right after getting off from one of the marathon gossiping sessions with Rita, she was in a very negative mood. She never felt happy after ending a conversation with Rita, even though she enjoyed the gossip.

Lynn also realized that her weight was out of control, her bills were piling up, and she never had time to cozy up with a good book. When she did an assessment of her time, she realized she was spending, on average, an hour and a half a day on the phone gossiping with Rita. She was totally neglecting her CTLAs of family, self-improvement, health, and other personal relationships.

She realized gossiping wasn't doing anything to improve her personally. She was wasting her time away by investing in these empty, negative conversations with Rita. Lynn decided to limit her discussions with Rita to no more than twice a week. She used the extra time to start a daily exercise routine, and within two months, she had lost ten pounds. She felt more attractive and happier about herself. This made her spend even less time talking to Rita. Rita finally got the hint and stopped calling altogether. Lynn didn't shed any tears. She was thankful she had redirected her time to focus on something that could improve her life instead of tearing others down.

One of the worst places to get entangled with a gossip is at work. A woman who does this is putting her livelihood at risk by providing personal information that could be used to damage her reputation. This is especially harmful if the woman has a position of authority. If subordinates get a hold of gossip about a manager, they could use it to openly disrespect the manager. This would undermine her authority, leaving very few recovery options.

Bridgett was an executive in a high-pressure job. She worried constantly that her peers were undermining her. She had always been a private person. In the past, her mother and high school friends had belittled her, so she really didn't trust people much, especially other women.

Unfortunately, Bridgett was hit by a devastating divorce. Her husband had been her support system, but now he was gone. She felt alone, without anyone to talk to. Around that time, Jane, an outgoing woman at work, invited Bridgett to meet her for coffee. Bridgett felt she should take Jane up on her offer and agreed.

Jane was a real talker. She knew a lot of people and chatted away. This provided Bridgett with a diversion from her own problems. Feeling vulnerable because of her divorce, Bridgett opened up to Jane about the reasons for her split, which weren't very pretty. Bridgett felt Jane was a good listener who offered heartfelt suggestions on what to do.

What Bridgett failed to realize was that Jane was an incorrigible gossip. She secretly fed Bridgett's problems to her other friends and coworkers. Bridgett was in a position of authority, so Jane's friends were delighted to hear of Bridgett's misfortune.

After a while, Bridgett began to notice that people at work responded to her differently. She also put two and two together, realizing that most of the people who were acting differently toward her were in Jane's circle. Though it was late in the game, she noticed that Jane gossiped about others incessantly, and Bridgett started feeling uneasy. She knew deep inside that if Jane could talk so freely about her other friends, she could very easily talk about her. The downside was that Bridgett had already shared personally damaging information with Jane. Now, she had to work on repairing the damage Jane had probably done to her. Bridget decided to distance herself from her new friend.

Bridgett learned a powerful lesson. When you are going through a tough personal period, share your troubles in a safe environment. Divulging information to a coworker, even if she is a "friend," is risky at best. The best place to share is outside of work with a tried and trusted friend or a competent counselor. At a time when Bridgett needed her job, she allowed Jane to contaminate that environment for her.

Another way gossip can hurt someone at work is when a woman contributes to the rumor mill and it gets back to one of her superiors that she is discussing unfounded information. This will create an air of distrust with people who could otherwise have promoted her.

Tattletales aren't just limited to elementary school. There are tattletales who take their skills right into adulthood. They can be found in many places—at family gatherings, in church, around neighborhoods, and at work. Tattletales in the workplace are very dangerous. They have an agenda to further their careers at the expense of their colleagues, and these tattletales feel very little guilt about undermining others. They exhibit extreme loyalty to one person—their boss—and no loyalty to anyone else. In their minds, there is no room for an alternative viewpoint other than the one that their manager has, even though he may be wrong.

Pam was a tattletale. She was the administrative assistant to an executive with a staff of about fifty people. The executive had come in with a very dictatorial style but often brought Pam gifts and flowers. As far as Pam was concerned, the executive was great. Pam didn't really care how her manager treated her people. The only thing that mattered to Pam was that she was well taken care of.

Whenever one of the staff confided in her about real problems they were dealing with, she would run back to the executive and spill her guts. The executive would proceed to punish or sometimes fire the supposed "troublemaker" Pam had ratted on.

Soon, the staff got hip and realized they couldn't trust Pam. They stopped sharing information with her other than ordering supplies. Ironically, Pam didn't understand why the staff had suddenly stopped including her in their coffee breaks and inviting her to the after-work get-togethers. They feared her, and rightly so. No one wants to innocently make a comment in what they think is a safe forum just to have it used against them later.

Tattletales have very few "real" alliances at work. When the executive to whom they have hitched their career wagon begins to move, they move right along in step. In fact, they almost have to, since nobody else trusts them. If the executive gets laid off or sent to another company, the tattletale will be left alone to fend for herself. Being a tattletale is a risky investment. It works only if the executive keeps rising in the same company or is willing to take the person with him or her.

Unfortunately, the only way to identify a tattletale before being bitten is to ask someone whom you trust. Listen to what he or she says, but observe the potential tattletale's behavior to come to your own conclusion. With a tattletale, it's always better to be safe than sorry.

How does a queen deal with gossip? Easy. She just doesn't participate.

As we have discussed, most forms of gossip are destructive. The sooner you can remove yourself from a gossip's web, the better off you will be. The longer you stay, the more entangled you will become in the spreading of poison. Your own reputation may be damaged just because of your association with such loose-mouthed company. Being neutral around negative commentary about other people will enable you to maintain integrity and respect. Most gossips are damaged, empty people who try to attract attention by degrading others. Most people don't like gossips—they fear them; they use them. It's in a woman's best interest not to be one or deal with one.

Chapter 15:

Mule to Collective Perspectives

Most people are other people. Their thoughts are
someone else's opinions, their lives a mimicry, their
passions a quotation.

Oscar Wilde

Peer pressure is a common phenomenon that can
have a devastating impact on young adults. When a teen-
ager hangs out with her peers, they often try to influence
her dress, choice of dates, and extracurricular activities.
Many teenagers buckle under negative peer pressure be-
cause they want to fit in. Just like a mule conforms to the
desires of people around him, some women abandon their
natural tendency to conform to their peer group.

Although adult women have matured past some of
the pitfalls of hanging around their teenage friends, they
often succumb to peer pressure in their adult network as
well. Many women obsess about whether they are fat or
skinny, who has the cutest husband, who is engaged or not
engaged, or who has already had a baby. Some want to be
acknowledged as being more stylish than their friends. In

many ways, peer pressure is worse for adult women since they have more resources for competing with each other than they had as teenagers. Many adult women yield to the collective perspective of their friends or families.

Women can be hard on each other when one of them is different. For example, if a woman is a gifted athlete, other women may label her a lesbian even though she may be heterosexual. It is a way to isolate someone who may be different, who may perform better in some ways than others. It takes a certain amount of courage to be different. Some women haven't mustered that courage; consequently, they penalize the women who have.

Many women succumb to peer pressure in order to fit in and impulsively react whenever they feel they are not part of the crowd. This reactive mode in which a lot of women operate can have a negative impact on their lives. Rushing to do anything before you are mentally or financially ready can ruin your chances of long-term happiness. People who rush to conform are constantly on a treadmill, trying to keep up with their friends or family. Victims of peer pressure don't take the time to learn what they really want or what makes them happy. A woman's efforts to constantly keep up with others can result in a midlife crisis, credit debt, anorexia, or depression.

Laura was a young woman in her twenties who was greatly influenced by her peers' behavior. She and her best friend, Kiera, had attended college together. Both took jobs out of school and worked for similar consulting firms. They talked daily about the progress they were making in their careers and often met in bars to socialize after work.

After Kiera met a nice, single lawyer named Rick on one of their nights out, Laura constantly asked her about every date she went on with Rick. Laura was secretly trying to gauge how serious the relationship was between Kiera and Rick. She did not want to be left behind as "the single friend."

When Laura realized Kiera and Rick were getting serious, she started going through her Rolodex to see if she had any men friends with whom she could possibly develop a meaningful relationship. She locked in on one guy, Gary, and immediately called him up to ask him to meet her in the bar of an upscale, downtown steakhouse.

When Gary and Laura met, they engaged in catch-up conversation. Laura was silently bored, but she felt the pressure of Kiera's successful dating life weighing on her, and it caused her to subjugate her true feelings. She gave Gary the impression she was extremely interested in his career and asked him many questions about his dreams.

At the first opportunity, Laura called Kiera and shared all the details of their first date. Kiera seemed genuinely happy that the evening had gone well for Laura and Gary. During the conversation, Laura felt pressured to paint a more exciting picture to Kiera than what she really thought of the outing with Gary.

Within five months, Kiera and Rick had become engaged. This sent Laura into a tizzy. She rushed the relationship with Gary even harder. She scheduled more outings for the two of them and pressured him to introduce her to his parents. She was falling behind Laura, and that made her feel lost.

As Kiera started discussing her wedding plans, Laura felt increasingly left behind. She made sure she spent most nights at Gary's and constantly praised him. She felt she had to invest all her time with Gary because if she didn't he would never give her a ring.

Laura continued to pressure Gary to make a commitment, but he began to pick up on the transparency of her tactics and started to pull away. This sent Laura into an even greater panic, because she was falling further and further behind Kiera's timeline. After going on a couple of outings with Kiera and her fiancé, Gary realized what Laura was up to and dumped her.

Laura was distraught at the loss of her prospective husband and slid into a depression. She didn't even acknowledge she was trying to rush a marriage to keep up with her friend. The continuation of Kiera's plans made Laura feel more inadequate, and she immediately started to target another man as a potential mate.

How could a professional woman like Laura get so caught up in trying to keep up with Kiera? Basically, her validation came from how closely she could emulate Kiera's life. Laura was being a mule to Kiera's future and not carving out her own path.

There was something empty or missing in Laura's life because she didn't feel she was good enough unless she was emulating her friend's lifestyle. She did not take the time to examine herself to see what would make her happy. Instead, she took her cues for happiness from other people.

Many women like Laura think it is critical to fit in. They are concerned about what people think and don't want to be viewed as different. This often translates into these women constantly checking the pulse of what others think. There is also the constant bombardment of TV images that show us we need to exercise more, get better hair products, drive certain types of car, and dress our children in clothes from certain stores.

Laura was a robot of sorts, going through her personal life, imitating everything Kiera did. Laura didn't have any real dreams of her own, which made her adopt the dreams of others. The negative outcome of such behavior could lead her to make decisions that alter the course of her life in useless directions. She could find out too late that her choices have made her very unhappy because she reacted out of pressure.

Being a mule to someone else's thinking gives all of your personal power away. A woman who does this is in for a life of hell. When she makes these life decisions based on popular opinion and they go wrong, her friends will not accept responsibility. The mess will all be on her shoulders.

Another area in which some women become obsessed with how they are perceived is their physical appearance. The billion-dollar diet industry is an example of how much interest women have in maintaining a low weight. Sometimes, this shows up when women constantly try out one new diet after another. A dangerous manifestation of body image compulsion that primarily affects women is anorexia.

On August 17, 2008, Wikepedia stated, "Sociocultural studies have highlighted the role of cultural factors, such as the promotion of thinness as the ideal female form in Western industrialised nations, particularly through the media."

As everyone knows, the metabolism of most human beings slows down as they get older. Many women still try to maintain the weight they had in college or high school. To do this, they have to exercise more and more and eat less and less as they age. If this drive to be thin is out of control, anorexia could be the result.

Entertainment industry and tabloid magazines regularly portray skinny stars as anorexic. The September 2008 issue of *Fitness* researched the emotional roller coaster of clothes shopping. The article shows how much anxiety women have about their bodies in a private dressing room. How do you think these women feel when they get dressed to go to work every day? What could be the full range of their emotions when they dress to go out on a date? After having a baby, some women obsess about getting back to their pre-pregnancy weight within a very short time.

Why are so many women mules to their weight? They are bombarded by messages from the media that "thin is in." They also get messages from others who are similarly influenced by images in the media (e.g., movies, television, pornography, magazines, etc.) that suggest looking thin is a prerequisite for attractiveness, despite your age.

One example of a woman who has not buckled to this pressure is Queen Latifah. She has a lucrative cosmetic contract and is visually voluptuous. She will lose weight occasionaly, but not to an extreme. She is a real queen because she doesn't bend herself into a pretzel just to satisfy society's standards.

Unfortunately, some women who are mules to collective perspectives from their girlfriends bleed their need for approval to their unsuspecting children. Mothers force their kids to conform to collective perspectives at an early age by pressurising them to get unusally high grades so they can attend a particular private school; however, the mother's motivation is not always honorable. Often, the motivation is that someone else's son or daughter is going to a particular school, and some mothers feel their kids need to go there too.

The competitiveness doesn't stop at academics, though. Some women throw their kids elaborate birthday parties to outdo or replicate their neighbors' or friends' parties. The kids then begin to develop a sense of entitlement as if everything has to be big and expensive to be good. The wonderful value of spending a birthday with friends can be lost in this constant drive to keep up with the Joneses at any price.

Such extravagant parties can also damage kids who are attending because everyone is under pressure to buy a gift that will "wow" the assembled guests or be more expensive and fun than all the rest. The kid whose parents may not make a lot of money or who may have gotten into a private school on subsidies feels like an outcast at these functions. His or her parents don't have the financial resources to compete by presenting an elaborate or expensive gift at the party. The subsidy child might not have a stay-at-home mother who can run around for hours looking for the cutest, perfect gift.

Instead of developing their own lives, many mothers pressurise their kids to be something that doesn't fit their personalities or creative abilities. In this way a mother unconsciously tries to fill her need for recognition and acceptance in her own life.

Some contemporary women take their children to a homeless shelter or women's shelter to donate their old toys to kids in need. This often implies an overabundance of toys. Wouldn't it be better to prevent such overabundance by not buying too many toys in the first place—toys that will quickly bore the kids? Whenever a woman makes herself a mule to collective perspectives, despite her own desires, she is bascially handing over the control of her happiness to other people. When women also force their children to bend to collective perspectives, it is doubly tragic. By definition, being an adult means having the ability to make your own choices and live your own life. Being insecure and weak-mindedly seeking others' approval shows that, despite her age, a woman may not be mature enough to deal with the world on her terms.

Independent women take in helpful information from their environment and discard the rest. They create a life roadmap that works for them and does not kowtow to the the approval of others. Ellen DeGeneres is an example of a woman who literally dances to her own tune. Many years ago, she had a successful sitcom on television. The industry knew she was gay, but she played her character on the show as a straight woman for a while. Then, Ellen decided she wanted her character to come out on the show. It was a controversial move. Many were worried that her sponsors would cancel. Many critics said that if Ellen's true sexuality was revealed it would jeopordize her career. Ellen took the risk because the topic was personally very important to her. She also chose to come out for real on the Oprah Winfrey show.

After baring her true sexual identity, Ellen's show's ratings declined, and the show was cancelled. Ellen's career went into a lull for a while, but then she recovered with a wildly successful talk show, *The Ellen DeGeneres Show,* that launched in 2003. She was a queen for herself and other lesbians who were suffering from discrimination and oppression. She didn't let society's overall view define her actions. Ellen continues to be very popular because she is viewed as not only fun but authentic.

An earlier female pioneer of independent thought was Eleanor Roosevelt, probably one of the best known first ladies. She was married to a popular president and could just have coasted on his high approval ratings, then called it a day. However, Eleanor decided to set her own agenda to reach out to the poor and disenfranchised.

In the 1930s, Eleanor Roosevelt became a civil rights advocate at a time when it was not popular to do so. She established relationships with African-American civil rights leaders and was roundly criticized by white society. This criticism did not stop Eleanor though. She fought a symbolic battle to get Marian Anderson the right to sing at the Lincoln Memorial. She did more than throw fancy dinner parties and wear expensive clothes. Being a true queen to her ideals, she actively campaigned to make life better for those who had no voice at the time. When her name is mentioned in modern-day politics, it conjures up an image of courage and respect.

Angelina Jolie is another woman who has not lived her life to satisfy the status quo. She could easily have relied on her beauty to define her life and relationships. However, Angelina has pursued causes to advance human rights for those suffering all over the world. She has even put her money where her mouth is by donating millions of dollars to the oppresed and adopting children. As a single mother, she adopted children of different nationalities and made her own family. She didn't try to use her looks to build some picture-book family raised on little substance. She carries herself with dignity and expresses views that show she has done a tremendous amount of personal research into the issues that concern people in economically depressed countries. A man such as Brad Pitt, who is exceptionally handsome, was attracted to her not only by her looks but for her mind and her concern for those less fortunate. She clearly sets her own agenda. The UN was so impressed with her work that they appointed her their

Goodwill Ambassador. An ambassador may be a little different from a queen, but it is close enough.

What are the characteristics of a queen when it comes to dealing with collective perspectives?

- A queen has her own viewpoint about social issues.
- A queen converses with people from other cultures.
- A queen will listen to a person with religious viewpoints other than hers.
- A queen reads newspapers to keep up with current events.
- A queen, at some point in her lifetime, has held a view that may be perceived as controversial because it was the right thing to do.
- A queen not only says a cause is right but puts some of her time and money behind that statement.
- A queen can express her beliefs without shoving them down other people's throats. She knows that just as she has a right to her beliefs, others have a right to theirs.
- A queen has popularity that is based on something other than money and looks.

Examine your life and your current choices to see whether you made them because you wanted to or because others influenced you. Do you do anything that would be considered socially or morally important outside of raising your family? Do you participate actively in any charities or social causes to help others? Do you let others guilt you into believing what they believe or into taking on their opinions? If you answered yes to any of these questions, you may have some work to do to make the transition to queen status. The first part of change is knowing that there is something that needs to be fixed. Reaching out to help others may only cost you time, which is time well spent if it helps you develop your own independent thoughts.

Chapter 16:

Mule to a Bad Man

Love is supposed to elate you, not make you doubt yourself.

Tracy E. Hopkins

There is only one chapter in this book that focuses on men. That is intentional. Most books for women revolve around men—how to get them, how to keep them, how to make them happy, and so on. This book is meant to focus on what women need to do for themselves to improve their lives. However, it cannot be denied that men are an integral part of many women's lives, thus the need for discussion on being a mule to a bad man.

First, it would be helpful to define exactly what a "bad man" is. The term itself is open to many different interpretations. For the purposes of this book, though, let's discuss what qualifies a man as being "bad."

A bad man is one who is selfish. He generally puts his desires first, even if he has a wife and kids. He then expects them to adjust their lives to meet his needs. A bad man does very little to meet their needs other than paying bills, if he even does that properly. He is always twisting his family's life around the ascent of his career or the new business idea he has. He resents any time that is focused on the family needs instead of on him and his goals. Some would call this type of man a narcissist.

Another type of bad man is one who is physically abusive. If he hits you or your children out of anger, the man is bad, period. No childhood drama or work pressures can excuse this type of behavior.

Another type of bad man is one who is verbally or emotionally abusive. He doesn't take his wife or girlfriend's viewpoint seriously. He always finds a way to laugh at her and put her down. He belittles her intelligence and her ability to make adult decisions without his input. He also doesn't limit his abuse to comments about his partner's mental ability. He comments on her looks as well, sometimes calling her ugly, fat, sloppy, old, too pale, too dark, and so on. Most people, other than the wife, are unaware that this man is such a misogynist because his verbal putdowns of her are usually done behind closed doors. However, there is a type of verbally abusive man who will try to engender pity for himself by putting his wife down in front of family and friends.

Another type of bad man is the cheater. He behaves as if he is still single, even though he is married. He flirts with women whenever he gets the chance to prop up his insecure ego. He regards his wife and children as props he uses to create a façade of how he is an upstanding family man. He also enjoys the stability of family life but is unwilling to do what it takes to be truly loyal to them. This is a man with damaged self-esteem. Any woman married to this type of man will be subjected to pretty much the same behavior.

The economic loser is another type of man who is bad for a woman. Unfortunately, this is the type of man many women love to make excuses for. Some of these men can't seem to hold a job for long. They quit or get fired because of a lack of commitment or a caustic personality. Some of these men spend all their available income on toys and material things to keep up with their friends. Investing in household needs, kids' education, or retirement for him and his wife is last on this type of man's mind. One other type of economic loser is the type who is perfectly fine with his wife working two jobs or being the primary breadwinner and paying most of the bills while he settles for a mediocre job that allows him plenty of time to watch television. While she gets stressed out juggling all of her work pressures, he gets plenty of rest and entertainment.

Another type of bad man is the liar. He is not to be confused with the cheater, who also lies to maintain his double life. A liar may not cheat, but he lies about major things that concern his partner and family. He lies about how his job is going. He lies about his future career prospects. He lies about the history of his family relationships. He lies about his past. He lies about how he spends money. He lies about the state of the family's financial affairs. He often uses these lies to portray himself in a positive light. The lies try to mask his poor decision-making capabilities by portraying an image that he and his family are more successful than they actually are. This man never operates in reality. Any woman who has her life intertwined with his is putting herself and her children at risk of a future disaster.

The last type of bad man we will highlight is the type who is cold and uncaring. Secretly, this man is emotionally shut down and has a problem bonding with most people, even his children. He shows very little emotion, affection, or understanding towards others. When a woman runs into a problem and needs a sympathetic ear, she has to turn to friends and family because this man is "not available" or gets annoyed any time he has to listen to her.

Bad men prefer women who are "mules" versus women who are "horses"—those who might be one step closer to being a queen. Women who are mules allow themselves to be manipulated and controlled. This allows men with weaker self-esteem to feel comfortable because they have a woman who is highly predictable. He doesn't have to worry about her challenging him often.

Now that we have defined the key types of bad men women make themselves mules for, we need to examine exactly how this tends to happen, as well as some of the effects of linking up with these men on a woman's long-term emotional and financial health.

Deandra was married to Whitney, who had earned an undergraduate degree in biology. She was a nurse. They met each other when they were seniors in college. They subsequently dated and got married. After both started their first jobs out of college, Deandra quickly got pregnant. Whitney thought she should have waited longer, but he had to accept the situation.

Whitney decided he wanted to go on to medical school, which would require them to move. Deandra wasn't too thrilled with that idea. She wanted to start putting down some roots because she had been the product of a single-parent mother who had struggled. She voiced her opinion to Whitney, but he wasn't really concerned with what she wanted. He packed up and moved to start the first semester of medical school. She stayed behind to work for a year, all the while taking care of their young child alone and sending money to Whitney.

When things became overwhelming with the long work hours and daycare, she decided to move in with Whitney so the family could be together. This would allow Deandra to get some help in caring for their young son. Deandra didn't realize it, but even when she was living with Whitney, she was still doing most of the child care with her young son because Whitney spent long hours on campus "studying."

Upon graduation, Whitney worked in town for a while and then wanted to move to take advantage of another opportunity. Deandra didn't want to move but followed her husband since this was his first job out of medical school. Whitney worked at this job for two years and then wanted to move again. Deandra was tired of moving and confronted Whitney about it. Whitney pretty much had a "take it or leave it" attitude.

Deandra was hurt and angry. She felt like she was just an add-on to Whitney's life. It seemed he was concerned only about his career and not hers or his child's life. She had made all new friends and felt welcome in the neighborhood. Because of her feelings of resentment, however, their marriage was tense. Since Whitney didn't give any ground, Deandra caved in and agreed to the move.

The new town was filled with older people. There were no young women or friends in the neighborhood with whom to have coffee or a social visit. Deandra had to pretty much focus her attention on raising her kids and working. It was a very lonely life compared to what she had enjoyed.

In all marriages, there is a lot of compromise. However, when one partner makes continual life changes and the other partner is expected to follow, this can wear on the health of a marriage. If people are selfish as singles, they often take these same narcissistic traits into a marriage. Some compromise is healthy, but if a woman is always compromising to accommodate a man's ego, she is making herself a mule to a selfish man.

And the damage doesn't stop with the woman if she is a mother. The kids are also unwillingly subjected to changes that may not be most beneficial to a healthy childhood. Some mothers, by making themselves mules, make their children mules as well. Every woman should have a line beyond which she will not compromise, even in a marriage. Deandra should have had that boundary, but she didn't. This enabled Whitney to constantly redirect their lives with little input from Deandra, who continued to be a mule to Whitney well into her late fifties.

Some men would compromise if their women stood up for their choices a little more. Other men wouldn't, and the marriage would simply end. It is an individual choice a woman has to make about the quality of life she thinks she can have. Many women let themselves become mules because they think their options are limited. They think they have to put up with unreasonable behavior because they believe no one else would marry them. This is usually a false belief and a result of damaged self-esteem.

Ann was such a woman with damaged self-esteem. She had lost her mother as a young child and felt abandoned. Being overweight, she didn't feel she could hold onto an ambitious or successful man. Thus, instead of losing weight to become more confident, she went after men who had something missing. They either had no job, no car, or no apartment. This allowed them to be more dependent on her, which temporarily allayed her feelings of abandonment. But this dependency on Ann caused her to overwork herself. The first long-term relationship she had was with Mark. He had worked for a responsible boss who would get him construction jobs frequently. However, Mark was lazy and unreliable. He began not showing up some mornings for the construction work. This prompted Ann to call his manager regularly to see if Mark had showed up for work. When he hadn't, Ann would hunt Mark down at his favorite hangout spots and push him to go in to work.

When a grown man needs you to prod him to do what he needs to do for himself and his family, he is not a man—he is a child. If a woman decides to date such a man and take on the responsibility of constantly having to oversee him, she is basically agreeing to be his mother. This means she has personal issues she needs to address.

The sense of abandonment Ann felt as a child pushed her to seek men she could control. Controlling them allayed her fear they would abandon her. When you have to motivate a man, you are playing both man and woman. This doesn't just drain a woman's energy over the long term; it also causes her to lose a great deal of her femininity.

Ann eventually became so fatigued by chasing after Mark that she dropped him. Unfortunately, she didn't address why she had picked a man like Mark, and she went on to pick another loser—Barry.

Barry was also in construction. However, he didn't have a car or a place to stay, so Ann agreed to find them an apartment. Barry was reliable when it came to going to work. This made Ann feel she had made a better choice this time around. However, Barry's peers easily influenced him, and they weren't as reliable. He did recreational drugs with them in secret.

This didn't seem to be a problem at first. Barry worked faithfully and put his money into their young household. However, as his friends progressed to harder drugs to still get the same high, so did Barry. Eventually, he became addicted, and when his life came tumbling down, he took Ann down with him.

What became clear to Ann was that she had a problem picking a grown man, as opposed to a boy, to date. She decided to seek counseling and do some of the inner work she needed. Her therapist helped her identify the root causes of some of her choices in men, which honed her ability to identify and pick reliable partners.

Some women are mules to a man in their youth and let him father their first child. However, when the pressure of parenting hits them and they realize the man is not a reliable father figure, they cut him out and move on to more reliable prospects. They are then able to pick a man capable of treating them with the care they deserve.

Rita grew up in a large but economically depressed southern town. All through high school, she dated a guy called Eric. They decided to get married when they were both sophomores in college.

Things were okay at first. Eric didn't like the student life, so he quit college to get a job. Rita continued on, though, and was able to finish her degree. She became pregnant and had a baby girl, Janie. Rita went on to get a job as a computer programmer at a large technology company and was paid well. Eric, who was working a blue-collar job, became insecure about not having finished his degree.

Rita was a valued employee and her company started flying her all over the country to consult on difficult problems. That's when Eric began to resent her success. He started exhibiting erratic behavior, hanging out with his old friends from high school again. He was irritable and aggressive with Rita, and then she began to see evidence of drug use.

Rita cared about saving her marriage and keeping the father of her daughter around. She also had to maintain her job despite all the stress. When she repeatedly confronted Eric about his drug use and behavior, he refused to listen. She suggested counseling for both of them, but Eric wanted no part of it.

When things didn't change, Rita asked her company for a transfer to another city, packed up, and left Eric. She relied on the supportiveness of her mother and was able to start her life over. She went on to meet George, an engineer at her company. He was hardworking, honest, and most importantly, drug-free. They dated and got married.

George proved to be a great father figure to Janie. He spent time teaching her his hobbies and helping her with her homework after school. George also took care of her and paid more than his share of the bills to keep the household running. Rita felt she had made the right decision for her and Janie. If she had stayed with Eric, he would have continued to drag their lives down.

Rita had the strength to do what she needed to do to take care of her and her daughter. She didn't let a youthful mistake become a lifelong tragedy. Rita transformed herself from being a mule to a bad man into a queen to a good man.

Why are some women able to leave a bad man before permanent damage is done while other women cannot?

The women who take the action required to get their lives back on track usually have a combination of self-esteem and some external support system, such as family or friends. This gives women the strength they need to make the difficult choice of leaving a bad partner.

The following are the characteristics of a woman who can leave a destructive relationship and reclaim her life:

- First and foremost, she has a job of her own.
- She doesn't expect somebody else to rescue her.
- If she has kids, she puts the kids' well-being and emotional health above her own needs and insecurities.
- She believes deep down she is attractive enough to get another man.
- She has reliable family members or friends who can help her transition and deal with the sense of loss.
- A woman who transforms herself into a queen after a bad relationship is not afraid to relocate if necessary to jumpstart her life again.

Depending on a man for your total happiness and well-being is risky at best. Even a woman who is happily married needs to have a plan B if things suddenly change with her mate. A queen always looks for a peaceful environment for herself and her children. We all make mistakes, but the key is not to stay stuck in them, to learn, and to move on to more nurturing surroundings.

Chapter 17:

Mule to Anti-Intellectualism

I think there's a difference between ditzy and dumb. Dumb is just not knowing. Ditzy is having the courage to ask.

Jessica Simpson

Dumb blonde. Bookworm. Airhead. We have all heard these terms used to describe a particular woman's intellectual ability. In society, women are usually placed in one of two categories, whether they like it or not: beautiful or smart. Which category is most advantageous for a woman to be in? Some would say that being beautiful can yield greater financial benefits, such as marrying well or being a movie star. The popularity of fashion magazines, plastic surgery, and diets would seem to confirm this. However, feminists groups would argue that intelligence is the most critical asset for a woman to possess. They feel it allows her to earn a living and be independent. Let's do some analysis that will allow you to come to your own conclusions.

Some women feel they have to invest in increasing their brain power because the beauty option may not be there. What kind of women make up this category? Women who are overweight may believe they have to be smart and work hard to get ahead in the workplace. They may think they cannot marry rich and will therefore have to provide for themselves. Sometimes, there is a cultural component to a woman choosing to invest a lot in education. For instance, if she is African-American, she may not believe as much in the "Prince Charming to the rescue" theme. She may have grown up seeing that her mother and aunts had to work to take care of their families. She may not believe that the option of relying on her beauty is a safe one. Unattractive women may also feel they have to have some academic achievements behind them, since their looks aren't there. Family members and friends growing up may have confirmed this notion with cruel comments about their looks as well.

At the other end of the spectrum, beautiful girls get a lot of positive reinforcement growing up. They are always hearing comments like "you're so pretty" or "you're so cute." The continual focus on looks, along with the positive reinforcement that goes with it, will basically teach an attractive child that all you need in life is to look good or dress well.

So, when do beautiful girls get a wake-up call and realize that investing in their looks to the detriment of all else may have been a bad decision? It can come when a marriage breaks down and they have to support themselves and their children. It may come when their opinion is never respected in adult discussions. It may come as they get older, when their looks fade.

Jennifer was such a girl. She was Puerto Rican, beautiful, and had a sparkling personality. As she grew up, everyone catered to her. When she became a teenager, men became particulary interested in her and always did things for her. She met a promising young man in high school and they married young. She went to college and earned two degrees but felt like she didn't have to use them. Her husband, Robby, made good money working on teams building shopping centers. They had a pretty good life.

Once children came along, Jennifer got deeply into being a mother and quit giving Robby all the attention he was used to. Robby had chosen Jennifer because she was beautiful. He felt that, because of his looks, he deserved someone just as attractive. Looks were his most important criterion. However, when Jennifer quit doting on him and focused instead on her two young children, Robby became frustrated and began to cheat.

He met an attractive dancer and they began an intense affair. When Jennifer found out, she confronted Robby, and he moved out. He had found someone younger, prettier, and more energetic than Jennifer. After the divorce settlement, even with alimony and child support payments, Jennifer's lifestyle dropped dramatically. She had let her college skills atrophy, so she couldn't find a job that paid well and would also allow her to spend time with her kids. Finally, the expenses got to a point where she had to seek public assistance.

However, the men who had always given her attention were now either married or had other issues. She didn't want to hook up with someone just because he had money, especially if he didn't always treat her well.

With all of her good intentions, the pressure of being a single mother began to tell on Jennifer. She barely had enough to pay bills and was always struggling to shuttle the kids to and from activities. The busyness became overwhelming. She finally went to school at night to get a certification in the investment industry. She was able to get a job based on her looks and ability to speak Spanish.

Things seemed to go well at first. Everybody treated her well in the firm. Unfortunately, when she was unable to bring a lot of new business in and provided confusing information to customers, her management team took her less seriously. They stopped handing her clients, and she began to feel isolated. Eventually, she quit the firm to start her own business. However, she didn't do her research into the viability of her customer base, and now she is losing money.

Jennifer is an example of someone who skated by on her looks. She found a way to squander the educational opportunities she had obtained because she was so used to men doing things for her. Relying on looks is like an addiction. Once you start doing that as a young child, the positive reinforcement makes a woman want to keep doing it right into adulthood. Despite their best efforts, women's ability to rely on their beauty for their livelihood has an expiration date.

Many Hollywood starlets have run into similar roadblocks—Joanne Woodward, Farrah Fawcett Majors, Gena Davis, and others. When they were younger, looks got them a lot of their parts, but when they grew older, the movie industry wasn't as kind. This happens not only in Hollywood but in society generally.

Hayden was an example of a woman who relied too much on her looks. In high school and college, she looked like a young Claudia Schiffer. She got invited to all the cool parties where there was an abundance of booze and drugs; when she went off to college to major in education, she took her partying habits with her. She couldn't concentrate on her English and math studies because she was partying too hard. When her parents got her first two semesters' grades, they knew she hadn't been studying and they cut off her money. Guys were eager to study with her. She tried this, but her focus just wasn't there. After another semester of bad grades, she had to drop out.

With no financial support from her parents, Hayden began waiting tables. By earning enough tips and taking out her own student loans, she returned to school. However, she had to change to a simpler major because she was working so many hours and didn't have as much time to study.

Hayden learned early in life that it is dangerous to rely exclusively on your looks. Even though her looks brought guys in and made her popular, she still needed to study and do her own work. The guys couldn't take her tests for her.

One trick used by beautiful people who don't invest much in expanding their minds is getting other people to do stuff for them. Many of them have superior manipulation skills. They have been good at getting other people to do things for them ever since they were children. Just like the owners of mules, some attractive women are skilled at getting other people to do the heavy lifting for them.

Since a lot of men desire the attention of a beautiful woman, some beautiful women specifically target them. They hone a bubbly personality to artfully persuade men to remove roadblocks for them as well as provide them with opportunities they may not have truly earned.

Everyone has probably worked with a beautiful woman who didn't have many skills and wondered how she got hired. Everyone else ends up pitching in to do their work while these beautiful women smile and make excuses.

Kay was such a woman. She was blonde with nice blue eyes and a shapely body. She was always perky and talkative, so men enjoyed having conversations with her. A large corporation hired her at a nice salary after she charmed her interviewer at a career fair. In her new environment, she had female as well as male coworkers. Many of the females were from good MBA schools and worked very hard on the development of their product. She quickly learned she had much more leverage with the men than the women. However, the women in the environment noticed that although Kay did a lot of talking, she hadn't learned the product lines well enough to discuss improvements during their brainstorming sessions. They quickly began to exclude her from the meetings they had scheduled, unless the men on the distribution list raised objections.

Kay would sit in meetings and listen to the men's opinions. She would absorb any big words or new concepts they used to describe their products and would simply repeat them in subsequent meetings. Amazingly, this worked for about a year and a half. Then Kay's male manager got promoted to another position. He was replaced with another male who was young and ambitious. He quickly sized Kay up and viewed her as dead weight. The feedback he received from her coworkers corroborated his initial opinion. He found a politically correct way to transfer her to another department and get her out of his hair.

Kay continued to be bounced around from department to department. This did not cause her to work harder and learn new skills and products, though. She made friends with a manager who was blinded by her personality, and she asked him to give her a job in his department. His group was considered a maintenance group and was not in the limelight, but it provided Kay with a safe place to do nothing.

She stayed in her new department for a few years and let what little skills she had decay. When the company ran into tough times, her manager was retrenched. The new manager went through the department and quickly asssessed who the valuable employees were. Kay was soon retrenched.

Kay's story illustrates how relying on looks instead of continually learning can place a woman in a perilous situation as far as earning potential. However, in today's society, learning too much can be dangerous too. Some women may invest too much time in working hard and too little in improving their looks.

Ariel was this sort of woman. She studied hard in high school and got a scholarship to college. Her parents always told her good grades were the key to getting a top job and having a successful life. What they said was burned into her brain. She went to college and invested nearly all of her time in studying. She didn't date and never went to parties where she could have networked and honed her social skills.

Another thing she did to her detriment was to not lead an active lifestyle. She studied at her desk, in the library, and on her bed. To save time while studying, she would buy junk food to eat in her room or on the go. During college, her weight quickly ballooned by fifty pounds.

Though her GPA was one of the highest among her classmates in business school, when she began interviewing at the career planning and placement center, she noticed some disparity between her GPA and those of her competitors. Some of her female classmates with lower GPAs, though, would get invited to a second round of interviews and she wouldn't. She couldn't understand why, since her GPA was higher than theirs.

She eventually got two job offers, but they were not the kind she expected. She had majored in business marketing and wanted to work with advertising teams to present ideas to customers. Both jobs she was offered involved generating ideas, but the structure required that the manager or other team members would present her ideas.

She accepted the best of the two jobs and hoped that things would eventually change. Her manager liked her and gave her constant work. However, she was rarely asked to go to social functions to which other team members would be invited to promote products. She quickly realized she was being pimped. Her peers wanted her to generate all the ideas, but they would then take them and promote them to customers, allowing themselves to look good. She was just a behind-the-scenes player that none of the bigger accounts or customers knew. The company was putting her in a position where she was contributing little to her CTLAs of health, personal relationships, or self-improvement.

Fortunately for Ariel, she was a quick study. She looked at the type of people who were being assigned the large accounts and meeting with the customers. They were thin, well-dressed, and very articulate. She decided to make a change to get access to some of the broader opportunities. She joined Weight Watchers and started attending a local chapter of Toastmasters.

She approached her management team about career growth that would involve more customer interaction and networking opportunities. She gave them three months to make changes. When her current management came up with several excuses about why it was taking so long to give her a new assignment, she interviewed, got another job offer, and moved on to another company that put her out front.

Ariel was able to use her brain to study the attributes marketing managers used to choose who to give client-interfacing assignments to. Being a strategic thinker, she realized she had to discard the old notion that high grades and hard work alone would guarantee her success. She also had the confidence to realize that if her current management team didn't believe in her abilities, she could believe in herself enough to move on.

Women who depend primarily on their looks to get ahead are investing in a shaky strategy for the future. Being unsure about your discipline or the current state of affairs in the world might seem cute to some men over the short run, but in the long run these men grow tired of such women and discard them. This happens at work and in women's personal relationships as well. A queen never lets her mind grow stale. She invests time in learning so she can have something relevant to say to all the important people she will eventually meet.

The following are the characteristics of women who carry themselves like intelligent queens:

- They study and have a field of specialty about which they are knowledgable and proud.

- They are constantly learning to improve upon their knowledge base by reading, attending seminars, and having discussions with other intelligent people.
- When they get into a negative work or marriage situation, they can think and problem-solve their own way out of it.
- They know how to leverage outside resources but don't totally rely on them.
- They use a combination of attractiveness and smarts. They never count on just one of these attributes to get them through.
- They read books and travel to increase their exposure and experience.
- They don't whine about how they are not getting fair treatment in life. They analyze the situation to see what actions to take to change their circumstances.
- Their talk focuses not on gossip, celebrities, fashion, and beauty products, but on the practicalities of everyday life and relevant issues concerning progress in the workplace and domestic life. Importantly, people take their advice.

Adult women have to accept that looks run out, especially after a certain age. Even the beautiful ones need something to fall back on. Kimora Lee Simmons, Heidi Klum, and Cindy Crawford are three beautiful women who used their brains to learn new industries in order to create business empires. None depended on their looks and modeling earnings to secure their or their family's future. Take a page from their book and make yourself adaptable and your mind versatile. This will help ensure the royal future you deserve.

Chapter 18:

Mule to Phoney Hope

There is only once cause of unhappiness: the false beliefs you have in your head, beliefs so widespread, so commonly held, that it never occurs to you to question them.

Anthony de Mello

Hope is what keeps people going. It is the belief that there can be a good outcome to a bad circumstance. Hope for a better life now and in the afterlife is the essential principal for many global religions. Hope motivates change. When people feel there is no hope, they tend to give up and become bitter over time.

Unfortunately, like a mule, many women can spend their lives being patient under the pressure of heavy weights, with little evidence of progress. They endure the burden and give up their own comfort with less of a fight, hoping for a good outcome. They are essentially mules to phoney hope. What is "phoney hope"? When a person believes in a positive outcome despite the fact that all the available evidence clearly indicates no change in the situation, that is phoney hope. For example, if a woman is married to a cheater who continues to cheat over several years and, instead of collecting her self-esteem and leaving, she continues to whine to her friends and family, hoping he will wake up and be faithful one day—this is also phoney hope. Another example is when a woman has been passed over for a promotion time and again, despite having put in an impressive performance. She doesn't change jobs but just sits where she is, hoping management will wake up one day and treat her fairly. We'll examine some of the reasons why women can unknowingly become mules to unjustified optimism.

Most women are raised to believe in fairy tales. Many believe they will meet a handsome guy and bring up great kids in a beautiful house. This comes from years of watching television and expectations being placed on them by their mothers. Most of the stories kids see in cartoons and childrens' books have happy endings. Frequently, parents try to protect their children by shielding them from unhappy circumstances. When kids are young, parents also have to instill the skill of decision-making in their children. This will enable them to deal with difficult or unclear situations. Some parents do this better than others. The ones who do it poorly may do so for myriad reasons. Some may not know how to make good decisions themselves and therefore pass the habit of indecision on to their children. Others may subconsciously want to impede their kids' decision-making ability to make the children more dependent, thus giving themselves greater control. When parents deny their children the chance to make good decisions, they are setting them up to be victimized by people and organizations.

Bernice was a woman who was a mule to phoney hope. She grew up watching soap operas with her mother, who was a single parent. She was a beautiful, smart woman of biracial heritage. Sometimes, she had problems seeing which group she fit into. She and her mother placed a high value on education as a way to a more prosperous life. Bernice went on to college to earn an undergraduate degree in business. There she met Frank, who was an engineer. Frank was attracted to her and they began to date. Her mother encouraged her, because she had raised Bernice alone and thought having a husband was the most important thing in the world.

Bernice and Frank continued to date and soon became engaged. There were early signs that Frank had anger issues, though. He would get impatient with Bernice when she was slow to make a decision. He often became moody. Bernice thought this was typical behavior for a man, since she didn't have an actual father as a male role model on whom to base her feelings.

Bernice and Frank graduated from college and started professional jobs. They got married. They were optimistic about the great lifestyle they would enjoy by combining their two professional incomes into their new household.

Unfortunately, Frank still had unresolved anger from being belittled as a child. After two kids came along and job pressures started to hit, Frank began taking his frustration out on Bernice. He began physically abusing her. She would reach out to friends for help, and they would offer help, but Bernice would not leave. She would tell her friends she was praying for an answer, but she would not take any personal action.

Frank would always calm down after his outbursts, and that would give Bernice hope that her domestic life would improve. Bernice was a mule to the false hope that Frank would realize the value of his family and straighten up. But he never did, and Bernice continued to stay, making her a mule to his unpredictability.

Bernice continued to use poor judgement. Already in a bad situation, she had two more kids. Despite the professional jobs she and Frank held, Bernice's choice to continue to enlarge the family put more economic strain on an already fragile situation. Because Bernice was unwilling to face the truth about the person she had married, she subjugated herself and her children to an abusive environment. Though there was turmoil at home, she continued to put on a façade that she was a happy, up-and-coming professional.

Some women, such as Bernice, rely solely on prayer to rescue them from a bad situation without doing the hard work necessary to extricate themselves from the mess they're in. Instead of assessing the problem, developing solutions, creating a plan to execute the solution, and moving forward, they hope that God and everyone else will do the heavy lifting to move them out of their predicament.

Many women, such as Bernice, cling to unrealistic ideals about how the world works. Many believe education will be the ultimate solution to most problems. Some believe that if they can just get married, everything will be perfect. Some young, single women believe in the ideal that marriage is continually romantic. To be fair to these women, some of their beliefs in utopian relationships come from being conditioned by culture as a whole. For example, many women place much value on receiving a box of candy on Valentine's day from their man without realizing that a dedicated man should show real commitment every day, not just on one day.

Prior to getting married, some women believe the bigger the engagement ring the more intense the love. To many, a smaller ring symbolizes a smaller amount of love. Women who try to impress others at the expense of financially chaining themselves to an unhappy job or loveless marriage often make themselves mules to a skewed sense of what's important. Such behaviors include having a big wedding, helping pay for a bigger ring than her man can afford, or financing an elaborate funeral to show how much someone was loved. Women who are mules to the impression that is being created are generating expenses they can rarely afford. It is a well-known fact that women generally make less than men for performing the same jobs. Some women spend a lot of their discretionary income on one-shot deals to make an impression and, due to unequal pay, they can afford that behavior far less than men.

Abusive relationships are just one area in which women can have the phoney hope that things will get better on their own. Health issues are another area where women can have a false sense of hope that the body will magically heal itself. Instead of listening to the body's symptoms, some women are so concerned with doing high-pressure assignments at work or taking care of family members demanding attention that they neglect their own physical self-care. Some harried women neglect the CTLAs of health and self-improvement altogether to cater to others' needs.

Many annual checkups are recommended for women, and the number increases as they get older—pap smears, mammograms, physicals, cholesteral checks, diabetes tests, blood pressure screenings, and so on. However, in today's rushed society, many women who work don't take the time to get these tests. They somehow think they can put these off. There are projects at work that are so "critical" these women need to forgo health checks in order to hold the all-important conference calls.

Women put their health needs on hold to work on things they have given a higher priority than themselves. These women believe their families or jobs can't do without a couple of hours of their time while they go to the doctor. What do these women think would happen if they were suddenly diagnosed with breast cancer and had to go through chemotherapy? Would the job stop and wait for them? Would their kids or family members stop needing and asking for things? The answer is clearly no. Women should put their self-care first. Having to take off a couple of hours to do a preventive checkup is better than being out for months, or, worse still, dead.

Donna was one of these women who took care of everybody else but didn't take care of herself. She worked ten-hour days at work on high-pressure projects. She was the clutch person that her management would rely on to fix a mess someone else had created. She also had to do a lot for her mother, who was elderly and sick. To visit her mom, she had to drive an hour every weekend, and she would give her money for the week. Donna's church also seemed to constantly need her attention. They always asked her to volunteer for some mission or meeting group. Donna would always dutifully participate. Because she had great project-management skills, they always asked Donna to pull together an outreach project or church program.

Donna knew her life was too rushed but felt she was young and could keep going at high speed for a while. All these people seemed to need her. Since she had no man, feeling needed felt good even though it was making her tired and caused her to crash when she got home late at night.

When Donna started having blackouts and the doctor couldn't diagnose a cause, the only thing Donna was concerned about was missing work. Her family called to check in on her, but no one else seemed to really have time for her. They put her name in the "sick and shut in" section of the church bulletin, but no one came to bring her food or stop by to see her.

Donna continued to hold onto the key projects at work until the blackouts increased and her doctor pulled her out of work for some mandatory rest. She received a couple of phone calls from concerned coworkers, but after a couple of weeks, these calls dropped off.

Donna's doctor finally diagnosed her as having Type II diabetes, which had been brought on by being overweight. When the doctor asked her about her diet, Donna had to admit that she ate a lot of fast food. She was always rushing to take care of a church group or conduct a meeting. This caused her to eat hamburgers, pizza, fried chicken, and other junk food. She secretly liked eating out because that was the one time of day somebody waited on her; it also allowed her to relax and catch her breath. Unfortunately, this habit was contributing to her obesity, which caused the diabetes. She realized that putting others first and hoping she would be healthy because she was young was being a mule to unrealistic hope.

She might have had phoney hope, but her body was tired and damaged. It gave her the message she had been unable to figure out, even with her advanced degrees. How can really smart, successful women be so stupid when it comes to their health? Easy—they put everybody first and themselves last. The human body is a robust machine. It can take a lot of abuse. Some women, however, push the body's ability to be resilient too far. Donna was lucky. Some women miss cervical or ovarian cancer or miss chest pains and have a heart attack, while others have headaches that go undiagnosed and turn into silent strokes.

Donna did take her doctor's advice, though. While she was out, she read up on the proper diet for a diabetic. She started grocery shopping and pre-preparing meals to eliminate high sugar and high carbohydrate foods. Donna lost most of the extra weight, and the diabetic symptoms disappeared. She tells many people that the blackouts revamped her life, for which she was grateful. She had assumed her body would keep going, no matter how much she abused it.

Even health professionals can neglect their bodies. Selena, for instance, was not just another successful woman who took her health for granted. She was an ob/gyn, constantly rushing to deliver babies at all hours of the day and night. It was hard to build a reliable eating schedule because of the unpredictable nature of her work. Also, like many professional women with high-powered jobs, she was single with no kids. For several years she had a relationship with another successful professional, but it failed due to the time they spent apart. Now, though, she was alone.

Being a doctor, she ate right most of the time. She was nice and slim. She also exercised by walking on a treadmill. Stamina was very important in the type of work she did. Because she was skinny, her sisters, who were all overweight, thought she was healthy. They often asked her to help them with their problems and their kids. Selena juggled work and family commitments for years without showing signs of wear.

Because she was living in a town with a booming economy, Selena had many young pregnant women as patients. Their living patterns were pretty much the same—they stayed at home and had babies while their husbands worked high-powered jobs in the corporate sector. Selena sometimes wished she had the lifestyle of many of her patients, but she had made different choices and felt she had to stick with the investment she had made.

Being a doctor, Selena had regulary scheduled her annual screenings. She thought regular checkups, along with her strenous exercise routine, would take care of her health. One thing she didn't think of preventing was the amount of stress in her life. Delivering babies was a very stressful job. Dealing with anxious, expectant parents-to-be had its own degree of daily stress.

Selena's family also imposed a certain amount of stress on her. Her mother was widowed and couldn't earn an income, which left Selena supporting her. She also felt obligated to pay for her sisters kids' tuition so they could attend good private schools. Along with all of this, she had huge student loans from medical school that she was still paying back.

When Selena found a lump in her breast and was subsequently diagnosed with breast cancer, she was devastated. Her doctor immediately started her on che-motherapy. Selena lost her hair and experienced severe nausea. Her family did come to take care of her for the two weeks she was recovering at home. Then the pressure to return to work hit and she went back, battling the nausea and other side effects of the chemotherapy while tending patients.

Selena did acknoweldge that because she was in good physical shape and ate a healthy diet, the most likely cause of her breast cancer was stress. She had read many studies indicating that breast cancer was more common in middle-class women, and that stress was a large contributing factor. A Swedish study by Dr. Oesteen Helgesson at Gothenburg University found that stress may double a woman's risk of developing breast cancer. His study was highlighted in a September 2003 article in WebMD:

> Although other studies have looked at the question of whether stress can contribute to breast cancer, those studies were based on reports from individual patients who were already diagnosed with cancer, and that could skew the results, says Helgesson, in an interview with WebMD at a European cancer conference. They found that women who reported being under stress had twice the risk of developing breast cancer as women who managed to stay cool, calm, and collected. This twofold risk held up even when they took into account other factors that might explain the increased risk for breast cancer, such as family history of cancer, alcohol use, body weight, smoking, and factors related to reproduction, such as the age when women first had their periods, the age they were when they had their first baby, and the age they were when they began menopause.

With all of her career success, why did Selena allow herself to become overburdened by taking care of others? First, being from a struggling African-American family, she was raised to have a strong sense of duty toward family, even when the burdens became unreasonable. That sense of duty wasn't limited to her family, though. Selena felt a strong sense of duty to her patients and didn't want to see them neglected while she took extended time off to tend to her own needs.

Selena had become a mule to her sense of duty. She bought into the phoney hope that exercise and healthy eating could override the detrimental effects of working in a stressful environment. Although the physical impact to Selena was obvious, there also had to be some emotional impacts of coping with all that stress. Possible side effects could be depression or unexpressed resentment.

Women have to face the fact that adult life is no fairy tale. They have to do their homework and see what risks their life choices imply. Believing in unrealistic ideals will only trap them in situations they are ill-prepared to cope with. Neglecting their health, staying in toxic relationships, taking on more responsibility than they can handle, and hoping that everything turns out fine is not a smart way to operate. Hope has to be constantly reassessed to make sure it is warranted and realistic.

So, how can a woman still remain hopeful without having blind faith? First, she can assess any relationship or envioronment she is in by asking the following questions:

- Does this person or organization give me positive encouragement?
- Does this person or environment allow me the time to take care of my own needs?
- Is this person or environment supportive of me when I am sick?

- Does this person or anyone from this environment call to check how I am doing?
- Does this person or environment cause me to spend more money than I would like?
- Does this person or environment leave me with a happy feeling after I have dealt with it?
- Does this person really listen, take to heart what I say, and act on suggestions for improvement?

If you answered no to two or more of these questions, you may believe in a person or environment that is not worth your faith. If you find this is the case, you can do the following:

First, talk to the person or manager in the environment and express your concerns.

If the person listens and takes action by modifying his or her behaviors to be more supportive, then the environment or person may be worth a second chance.

Second, if the conversation falls on deaf ears, meaning the person or manager disregards what you say, or even goes as far as making fun of you, just roll on and don't look back.

Some women believe in people who continually disappoint them without taking action or leaving. These women don't have the courage to acknowledge when they aren't being treated fairly. Sometimes, even when they acknowledge the poor treatment they may be receiving, they are too weak to take any constructive action to change their circumstance. What they are not coming to terms with is that people will take more from you than they rightly should get if you let them.

To be a queen as opposed to a mule, you have to stand up for what you think is healthy for you and hold people accountable when they give you less than that amount. Whining, complaining, and making excuses doesn't make people treat you any better. In fact, it usually accomplishes the opposite and makes them disrespect you. This sometimes can lead to them victimizing you more since you have exhibited powerless behavior. A little part of you gets eaten up by fear, day after day, until there is little of you left.

Queens, however, take responsibility for their own happiness. Fannie Lou Hammer was such a queen. She didn't sit around and whine that people were denying her and others the right to vote. She didn't let fear keep her from going after what she deserved. She said, "I guess if I'd had any sense, I'd have been scared—but what was the point of being scared? The only thing they could do was kill me, and it seemed they'd been trying to do that a little at a time ever since I could remember."

Fannie Lou Hammer went on to pressure President Johnson and Senator Hubert Humphrey to challenge Mississippi's anti-civil rights delegation at the Democratic National Convention. To save their own political careers, they were forced into a compromise that allowed African-Americans to be part of that delegation. Fannie Lou knew she could not believe in the phoney rhetoric that was being spouted by politicians. She had to take tough actions to ensure she and others were treated fairly when it came to the right to vote.

Like Fannie Lou Hammer, a queen doesn't make unreasonable demands. She makes demands for the fair treatment she knows she deserves. Queens also fight for the fair treatment of others, not just themselves.

The following are the hope characteristics of a queen:

- Believing in the good of people unless evidence shows otherwise.
- Not whining about being treated unfairly but taking action.
- Fighting for the fair treatement of others, particularly for those who don't have the strength, and not just herself.
- If the environment is toxic, a queen will work to change the environment but move on if her efforts prove futile. She is not waiting for a white knight to rescue her. She rescues herself.
- A queen's body is her temple, and she takes care of it as much as she takes care of others.
- A queen does not accept abuse for long.

Life is short. If you are running around letting your life being controlled by others, hoping for the best, you will be a fool in the long run. Hope is a great belief. It ensures action toward the future with the intention of receiving the good that life has to offer. However, unsubstantiated hope makes you a mule to the whims of others who may not deserve such a wonderful sense of belief. Hope is like a plant: it has to be continually watered and nutured or it dies. If people aren't cultivating your hope, pack up and move on to more fertile ground.

Chapter 19:

Everyone Needs a Stay-at-Home Support System

Little deeds of kindness, little words of love help to make earth happy like the heaven above.

Julia A. Fletcher Carney

Long commutes, remote access, Blackberrys, ten-hour workdays, rushed deadlines, and juggling kids between after-school activities—these are everyday demands for today's working woman. She often feels overwhelmed, and rightly so. If she is married, she may get some relief from her spouse. If a working woman is single, though, this pressure is amplified because there is no partner available to help.

Many women are raised to believe they can take care of all their personal and work matters. But in reality, this is a myth. Eventually, something will slip, and a woman's whole life will be thrown off balance. Many successful men have learned how to avert this disaster by having a stay-at-home wife. She runs errands, shops for groceries, handles repairmen, and pays bills while the man's mind is clear to concentrate on his work life. Realistically, when a professional woman is asked to compete against a man who has a lot of help at home, how can she? Some try to get around this by hiring nannies and maids. They can help out some, but there are still things in a house only a husband, a wife, or a live-in partner can do. That is why having a stay-at-home friend or retired family member may be the next best thing.

People who go to work in today's environment are often stressed and feel they don't have enough downtime. A stay-at-home friend or relative can help relieve some of the stress of juggling by being available to help out in a pinch. Their lives are less harried. They often will be in a peaceful state of mind that may be very calming to the frantic working woman. These women are queens because they have achieved a life that is more peaceful and doesn't rely on a broad range of people for their sustenance.

Henrietta didn't work because she had a disability. She had a master's degree and a sharp mind, but her physical disability kept her from being able to hold a full-time job. She had several single professional female friends who worked intense jobs. They would often call her for emotional support when they felt burdened. Some had kids they were taking care of alone. Some had high-powered jobs where they were constantly looking back over their shoulders, trying to shield themselves from workplace politics. Some had rocky relationships with men who had been unsupportive, so they were basically left alone to solve all their problems.

Henrietta had held marketing, career planning, and communications jobs in her past. She was able to give advice on how to handle tough career situations as well as ways to market new business ventures her friends may have been kicking off. She also had experience in hotline counseling and spiritual education at large churches. This allowed her to be empathetic and welcoming to women who felt beaten down and alone. Her professional friends also felt safe with her because she didn't have a judgmental attitude when she talked to them. Henrietta was available during the day and sometimes late at night for a calming word or intellectual discussion.

Relationships with Henrietta turned out to be great partnerships. The women she listened to would provide her with care and assistance when they had spare time or when she was going through a medical episode. She would provide them with emotional support and ideas that assuaged the stressful quality of life they experienced. Henrietta probably wouldn't have had the time or the mental clarity to support them if she had worked in a high-pressure job as well.

When a woman encounters a crisis in her life, having a retired or stay-at-home family member is essential for her to get her life back on track. Going through a divorce, coping with a serious illness, or caring for a young child are all examples of situations that may cause a woman to need a supportive person with extra time on his or her hands. Sometimes, men are reliable. Sometimes men are unreliable, though, and unfortunately there are a lot of women who don't have a man to count on anyway. So, a significant other shouldn't be a woman's only option for support.

Sheila, the mother of a young child, is one of those women who benefited from having a retired mother. Sheila was able to leave her abusive husband by moving near her mother. Since her mother was retired, she could babysit Sheila's daughter while Sheila interviewed for jobs. When Sheila realized the job she had found in a time of crisis was a dead end, she was able to go back to graduate school because her mother would pick up her daughter from school and babysit at night. Without that support system, it would have been very difficult for Sheila to change her negative situation into a more positive one.

Often, as a working woman, you need somebody to talk to who is calm and caring. Many professional women are so consumed by their own problems they can't give an earnest ear to someone else for very long. Retired or stay-at-home wives are not as harried, so they can provide a refuge from the hard-driving professional environments many women go to every day to support themselves and their families.

Lela liked to call her Aunt Mary, who was in her nineties and very kind. She had retired several years earlier and was available almost any time Lela called her. She had a wealth of life experience that helped Lela cope with difficult situations she encountered with coworkers or with the disloyalties of men in her life. Even though she lived out of town, Aunt Mary's home was open to Lela any time she wanted to visit and get some rest and *supportive* counsel.

Aunt Mary had endured racism, poverty, infidelity, health challenges, love, and family drama. There were not many situations Lela couldn't discuss with Aunt Mary because she had been through most of those situations. Her depth of wisdom was invaluable to Lela, as was her non-patronizing attitude toward mistakes.

Whenever her friends would flake out, Aunt Mary was always there for Lela to talk to. She provided Lela with a sense of stability that counterbalanced her chaotic job with crazy deadlines and little recognition.

When she was younger, Aunt Mary had been a fashion icon who had always acted like a lady. When Lela was confused about what to wear or how to act in a difficult situation, Aunt Mary could always give her some useful input. Lela was smart enough to invest in the CTLA of family through her relationship with her Aunt Mary.

All professional women need a supportive, wise woman in their life. It can be a mother, grandmother, aunt, or friend. No matter how professionally aggressive a woman has to be for her career, there is a feminine side that needs nurturing as well. This side manifests itself when there is a loss of love, death of a friend or family member, an illness, a loss of self-confidence, a bout of extreme criticism, a question about motherhood, and other life-changing events. Every woman needs a woman with whom she can have a heartfelt talk without the fear of being persecuted for having very human feelings.

Everyone needs somebody who is a cheerleader, somebody to bounce ideas off, somebody who can validate your life goals or help you identify short-term and long-term goals. If you don't have a spouse, you have to work harder to get this type of support system. Without a spouse, you have to build this framework yourself. You may have to convince yourself that you are smart or that you can reach a goal. You have to convince yourself to go on even when you are tired or lose focus. This is a tall order for someone to do alone.

Even for women with a bunch of so-called friends, such friends can be fickle—they may give partial support, but often it is inconsistent. Imagine a plant in a dark room receiving a small amount of light. It may survive, but it won't thrive. The plant won't reach its full potential because it does not have enough supportive light. This is a great metaphor for a person toiling alone. It shows how much harder it can be without a lot of support and encouragement. If there is someone encouraging you to believe you are the best and the brightest, then all you need to do is sit down and realize the vision. You have someone helping enhance what you believe is possible for yourself. This comes from your environment, the people around you who have the capacity to help you realize you can achieve a certain goal. If you don't carefully select your support system, you could be surrounded by people who have failed. If they are angry or insecure, you might end up embracing the attitudes of these people who have given up on their dreams.

You have to honestly and realistically assess the people around you. If you are in the company of people who espouse a negative philosophy, then you truly have to change that. The solution, if you do not already have a supportive person in your life, is to enter environments that have these kinds of people. You need to have a personal test, though, for identifying new, supportive people. The following are some questions you can ask yourself about friends:

- What happens when you ask this person about a goal? If the person highlights what's wrong with you instead of looking at what it takes to achieve the goal, the "friend" may not respect you. Avoid people who look for your flaws instead of your potential.
- Does your friend spend an inordinate amount of time highlighting others' shortcomings? If so, this is not the type of person you would want to have in your support system.

- Is the person very selfish? Self-absorbed people will drain you of your energy instead of giving you energy to help you focus on your vision. People who spend most of your conversation talking about their issues and rarely ask you what is going on in your life won't be really supportive. They will try to invest all of your time in their problems, and you won't have any time left for your dreams.
- Do these people have a bunch of problems? If you become their friend, their problems could eventually become yours. Such people may chronically mismanage their lives so the problems become continuous for you and them.
- Is the person narrow-minded? Narrow-minded people have a problem dreaming. They can't think outside the box in which they have been socialized. Therefore, they are likely to be critical or unreceptive to goals they may not have been exposed to. Thus, they can turn into dream killers.

When you are around people who don't believe you can achieve more than you already have, you can lose confidence and fail to achieve your true potential. By being around them, you are validating them in a way. However, if you are around supportive people, you are inspiring them and they are inspiring you. You are enabling them to be more inspiring. The synergies you create with them will create a stronger support system for both of you.

By the very nature of their circumstances, stay-at-home supporters have less chaotic lives. They deal with what goes on in their homes but don't have the stress of office politics. They often have the patience and wisdom it takes to be a really good friend. Therefore, if you have a retiree or a stay-at-home friend, you have a very valuable friend indeed.

Chapter 20:

How Do You Change If You Have Unknowingly Become a Mule?

Forget past mistakes. Forget failures. Forget about everything except what you're going to do now—and do it.

William Durant

What if you suspect that you have unknowingly become a mule in one area of your life? The following are some telltale questions to ask yourself:

- Do people disregard your opinion when you speak at a meeting?
- Do people ask about your interests?
- Do people want to tell you what to do without considering what other stuff you have going on already?
- Do you listen to people more than they listen to you?
- Do you financially support anyone who is not a child?
- Are you afraid to express an opinion that is different to those of your family and friends?
- Are you always tired from being overworked?

- Do you ever go out just to have fun, or are all your excursions purpose-driven?
- Does anyone in your life say things to you that make you feel bad?

If you answered yes to a few of these questions, you may be a mule in some aspect of your life. The real question is: can you change? The answer is yes. Change can be hard for most people, but it is doable. The following is the change formula derived by David Gleicher, Richard Beckhard, and Reuben Harris. It is used to gauge whether an organization has the ability to change, but it can also be applied to an individual's ability to change:

$D \times V \times F > R$

D = dissatisfaction with current circumstances

V = vision of how good things could be

F = first steps to make the change

R = natural resistance to change

The basic premise of this formula is that a person must have *dissatisfaction* at being a mule, a *vision* of how to be a queen, and the *first steps* or method for changing her behavior to prevent others from using her this way.

For example, let's say a woman is very overweight, and this impacts her self-esteem. She dates guys who don't treat her with respect because, in her mind, they are the only type of men who would be physically attracted to her. So, basically, she is allowing men to make a mule out of her. If the level of disrespect gets to a certain point, she may be so dissatisfied with the way men treat her she will lose weight to improve her self-esteem and thereby attract a better quality of man. She has to be able to *visualize* the quality of a man she could get, or the change may not be worth it to her (i.e., if she thinks all men are the same). She also has to know how to take the first steps to lose weight. Maybe she would use Weight Watchers or a personal trainer to start her weight-loss plan, but she has to know what *first steps* to take to start the weight-loss effort. So, to become motivated to change her eating and exercise patterns, her dissatisfaction with her weight has to be strong enough, she has to have a process for losing weight, and she has to have a hopeful vision of how good a man she could get with her new appearance.

Based on the premise of this change equation, any woman who realizes that she has become a mule has to be highly dissatisfied with this discovery and believe she can be treated better, as well as have a way to change her situation. Poor self-esteem is a key reason why women stay stuck in mule status. Deep in their subconscious, many women think they don't deserve better, so they don't make the change. They can't muster up the vision of how good their lives would be if they could eliminate all the users and exploiters. All they can see is that they would be alone. Unfortunately, for many women the fear of loneliness is worse than the fear of death.

Women who are mules are stressed out from too many burdens people have conveniently placed on their backs. They ignore their CTLAs and focus on those of others.

One key motivator for a woman to change from being a mule can be her children. If a woman has children, she needs to demonstrate through example that they can expect more than substandard treatment. A mule is a servant who basically feels powerless. So, if she wants to be more independent and increase the odds that her children will eventually become independent as well, she should want to change her mule status too. As the mother of female children, this is particularly important. When a woman is a mule, she is teaching a female child that she has no power and that it is acceptable and reasonable for her to be controlled by others who don't have her best interest at heart.

A woman who is a mule is also naïve, or a coward. At first, she can be naïve about how she is being used. However, she has to realize eventually she is being exploited. If she does nothing to change, she is, in fact, being a coward. Also, if she is a mule and does nothing, she is putting more value on other people's lives than her own. No one's life should be more important than her own. The Constitution says all men and women should be created equal. Some women play mind games with themselves by making flimsy excuses that justify the unreasonable behavior of others. There is no excuse for long-term, contemptuous treatment.

Unfortunately, some women have been programmed to sacrifice their happiness for the happiness of others. This involves them putting up with behavior that is disrespectful. Many times, a woman has to be extremely hurt to make a change. If there is something in her life that makes a woman painfully uncomfortable, she will often change. For example, when a man cheats over and over again, or when a woman is passed over for salary increases year after year, or her friends are always unavailable when she needs them to listen, she may finally wake up and make a change. These things can cause a woman to reach a breaking point where she says, "That's it. I'm done." The sad thing is how much of her life a woman can waste by taking so long to act. A queen does not respond this way. A queen sees disrespectful behavior and acts immediately. The longer a woman stays in a negative situation, the further away from a queen she gets.

When a queen is confronted by people or situations that try to take advantage of her, she speaks to the offender about her feelings of discontent. If the situation doesn't change for the better when she points out the discrepancy, she removes herself from that situation. A queen expects good treatment, and when it is not there, she extricates herself and moves on to fairer surroundings.

Chapter 21:

There is No Honor in Being a Victim

> When you don't know when you have been spit on, it does not matter too much what else you think you know.
>
> Ruth Shays

Most women have heard the word "martyr." The mere mention of this word brings up thoughts of honor and bravery. On November 4, 2008, Wikipedia defined a martyr as follows:

> The term "martyr" is most commonly used to describe an individual who sacrifices his life (or personal freedom) in order to further the cause of many.

Many think of a martyr as someone who devotes his or her life to help a worthy cause. Some modern women are confused about what constitutes a "worthy" cause. They think subordinating themselves to narcissists, self-absorbed friends, and controlling family members constitutes an honorable cause; however, most wom-

en who are victimized are not martyrs. Some willingly
participate in their self-destruction by not taking respon-
sibility. Some are even lazy and stubborn, holding on to
hope when it isn't warranted. They defend people who
knowingly mistreat them. Worst of all, many pass these
behaviors on to their children.

We all know them—women who have had lives as
hard as hell. They have troubled kids, cheating husbands,
low-paying jobs, and disrespect from all sides. Who wants
to be them? No one. Who celebrates them? No one. Well,
the question is: why do so many women struggle with
these problems? They let life happen *to* them. They let
people use them. But most importantly, they blame oth-
ers for bad things that happen to them. Like some mules
are victimized because they have uncaring owners, some
women are victimized repeatedly because they surround
themselves with awful people. Unlike mules, women can
choose who they deal with on a personal level. Some
don't exercise the right choices. They allow themselves
to become victims. However, there is no honor in being
a victim.

We all face adversity. Women generally face more
than men, due to sexism and earning less than men. Some
women had problematic early lives but did not let this stop
them from doing well for themselves and others. These
women are true queens. They didn't allow themselves
to become victims, but leveraged their hardships to push
themselves towards higher ideals. They also improved the
quality of life for many others. These women overcame
the negative voices that told them they couldn't reach
their goals. They overcame everything from sexism, rac-
ism, and family tragedies to achieve extraordinary results.
Best of all, these women did not hang on to the coattails

of a prominent husband. They dreamed their own dream. They carved their own path.

Nancy G. Brinker is not a name many women are familiar with. However, most women in America are aware of her sister, Susan G. Komen, who died of breast cancer. Nancy promised her sister, who was dying of breast cancer at thirty-six, that she would do everything within her power to end breast cancer. She established the Susan G. Komen foundation with a small amount of personal money.

To date, the Susan G. Komen Breast Cancer Foundation has raised more than 500 million dollars through the hard work of 75,000 volunteers. Nancy was able to take the personal tragedy of losing her sister to help women around the world fight the struggle against cancer. She didn't simply go to her sister's funeral, whine, and then go on with her life as if it were business as usual. She honored her sister's memory by helping millions of other women with awareness and resources to battle that deadly disease. Nancy G. Brinker achieved royalty status—she became a real queen.

Ann Richards was a feisty, intelligent young woman with lots of promise, who worked on Sarah Weddington's and Wilhelmina Delco's campaigns for the state legislature. She ran for a county commissioner seat in Austin, Texas, then went on to run for State Treasurer, and continued to become the first female governor in the history of the state of Texas.

All this did not come without a price. She openly admitted to struggling with alcoholism. She also survived a painful divorce. Ann did not let this stop her, though. She worked on a program to revitalize the slumping economy in Texas, and brought many corporations and jobs to the state. As a humanitarian, she reformed the Texas prison system and introduced a substance abuse program for inmates.

Her most famous moment was at the 1988 Democratic convention. She made a groundbreaking speech full of wit and wry Texas humor about George W. Bush and his privileged upbringing. She used her personal struggles to help others, including prisoners, women, and minority politicians, to lead better lives. Ann was not a southern belle but a regal woman with national influence.

Another woman who broke new ground was environmentalist Rachel Carson. Nowadays, everyone is talking about going green. Hybrid cars, recycling, and reducing global warming are all popular initiatives to save the planet. Before environmentalism became trendy, though, Rachel Carson was an advocate for conservation and environmentalism. She was a writer, marine biologist, and ecologist. Her early career as a biologist began at the U.S. Bureau of Fisheries. She went on to write several pamphlets on conservation.

After World War II, chemical pesticides were frequently used in the agriculture industry. In her work *Silent Spring*, Rachel Carson wrote about the damage these pesticides were inflicting on wildlife. This book's popular appeal contributed to the subsequent nationwide ban on the pesticide DDT. She is also credited with being the mother of the modern environmental movement. Many credit her as the catalyst behind the creation of the Environmental Protection Agency.

A queen takes stances that may not be popular. Rachel Carson spoke out against pesticides at a time when women were not praised for speaking out but for staying home and being someone's supportive wife. Rachel Carson's stance took guts.

She also made the world a safer place for future generations and animals by campaigning against the use of DDT and other pesticides. She fit the criteria of a queen by helping many others beyond herself.

Barbara Jordan overcame tremendous obstacles too. Her career grew in Texas at a time when racial tensions were high. She became the first African-American woman to be elected to the Texas State Senate in 1966, and then later to the U.S. House of Representatives in 1972. What is extremely remarkable about her achievements is that in 1973, she was diagnosed with multiple sclerosis. She persisted past the pain of the disease, and served on the House Judiciary Committee. In this role, she was part of a team that actively investigated and recommended the impeachment of Richard Nixon. She made a widely televised speech calling for Nixon's impeachment—a speech many people will never forget. Many of her allies did not know how severe her health problems were because she continued to be very successful. By not letting the handicap of a major illness stop her from achieving her goals, Barbara Jordan became a true queen.

Candy Lightner is a name few know as well. However, many know the organization she founded—Mothers Against Drunk Drivers. Before Candy's efforts, many people regarded drunk driving as something of a joke. When Candy's daughter was struck down by a drunk driver who was given a light sentence, Candy went into action. She coordinated meetings with several other mothers who had experienced the same tragedy. This group began using the media and lobbying Congress to enact stronger legislation against intoxicated drivers. Her work has honored her daughter's memory and prevented other mothers from suffering the loss of their children to drunk drivers. Candy was a queen who took action to improve others' safety.

Many have heard the epithet "the queen of daytime TV" used to refer to Oprah Winfrey. For two decades, she has run a very successful talk show. She is also widely respected for her intellect and good works. She has touched many women's lives with the eye-opening subject matter of her shows.

The story of Oprah's struggle as a minority woman growing up in the South is also well known. However, there are two things that make Oprah stand out in the queen category. First, she started a school for underprivileged girls in South Africa. Her goal was to create a safe place where these young girls could learn and excel, even though many politicians and celebrities had largely ignored Africa for years.

The beauty of the type of outreach she created is that she built a school that will employ and educate oppressed young women in South Africa for many generations. Her giving was not a one-shot deal, either. Although she had a busy schedule, she was also personally involved in the interviews and progress of the school.

The second thing that makes Oprah a queen is that she is willing to take risks. She appeared on *The Ellen DeGeneres Show* as Ellen's psychiatrist, discussing Ellen's lesbian orientation. Oprah took a lot of heat for this at the time but felt it was something she needed to do for her friend, Ellen DeGeneres.

Oprah also put her professional success at stake by endorsing Barack Obama for President. In the past she had not publicly endorsed any particular candidate, but she felt it was important to support Obama to improve the state of the nation. Yes, she is famous. Yes, she is rich. But there are a lot of rich celebrities who get to a point where they don't take risks that could threaten their career. Oprah is a queen for this reason.

The whole purpose of this book is to encourage women to stand up for what they need. Many women are socialized to put others' needs above their own. Having a high quality of life should be an essential goal of every woman's life. A woman has to fight for this quality of life. Often, it is not achieved without a struggle. If you have seen yourself in some of these stories and feel you may be a mule, hopefully this book will give you the blueprint to change your life and the way you are treated.

The Critical-to-Life Areas Every Woman Needs to Focus on are:

- Financial
- Work
- Spiritual
- Family
- Personal relationships/significant other
- Self-improvement
- Health

All these areas need constant nurturing. If a woman is neglecting any of these areas, she will not achieve the quality of life she deserves.

Others often have secret agendas, but you shouldn't let these drain your life energy. Invest in yourself so you can live the life you deserve and be a great example for your children and others.

Every time you feel someone is taking advantage of you, visualize a mule going up a hill with many sacks on its back. Visualize how the weary mule's legs will tremble under that burden, and threaten to buckle. Do you really want to be a mule to someone else's whims?

Live your life with a queen's honor and choices, and you will garner the respect of others. This respect will, in turn, ensure better treatment. Invest in yourself and have fun. That is what quality of life is really all about.

About the Author:

Lisa Blackwell is an experienced process-turnaround specialist. As an executive coach and professionally certified change agent, she has helped executives and other individuals achieve quantifiable performance improvement through identifying and removing wasteful activities that impact their work as well as their personal quality of life.

Ms. Blackwell has over fourteen years of expertise as an efficiency expert, leveraging both data analysis and soft skill improvement in highly effective methodologies, such as Balanced Learning and Process Excellence. She has been on leadership teams during initial rollouts of major initiatives requiring extensive culture changes at top Fortune 500 companies.